A Practical Guide to Integrating Generative AI into HR Management

This book is a practical guide to the integration of generative AI into human resources, covering use cases across recruitment, onboarding, training, and retention. It offers strategic guidance, ethical frameworks, and technical insights to help organizations deploy generative AI effectively while safeguarding fairness, privacy, and compliance. It covers AI-driven applications in talent acquisition, onboarding, employee engagement, career development, and decision-making while addressing key concerns such as algorithmic bias, data privacy, and regulatory compliance. With practical case studies and deployment templates, the book provides a structured approach to evaluating and integrating generative AI tools within HR systems. From resume screening to personalized learning paths and predictive analytics, this book bridges the gap between AI technologies and HR operations to help organizations build agile, ethical, and employee-centric workplaces.

- Examines generative AI's applications across recruitment, onboarding, L&D, engagement, and retention
- Provides strategic frameworks for integrating AI into HR ecosystems
- Includes case studies and practical deployment examples from real organizations
- Addresses key issues of AI bias, explainability, data privacy, and compliance
- Offers guidance on selecting and evaluating HR-specific AI tools
- Explains core AI concepts for both technical and nontechnical HR professionals
- Includes future-focused insights into AI-driven workforce planning and employee experience design

This book is for HR professionals, business leaders, AI developers, and organizational strategists seeking to understand, implement, and manage generative AI solutions in the HR domain.

Knowledge-based Engineering for Innovation

Nilanjan Dey
Professor with the Techno International New Town, Kolkata and visiting fellow of the University of Reading, UK

The series presents invaluable insights into knowledge-based engineering for innovation by investigating the role of emerging technologies like machine learning and artificial intelligence in enhancing knowledge management, data-driven research, knowledge-intensive applications, knowledge transfer, and related areas. By addressing the challenges and opportunities in this domain, the series aims to bridge theoretical and practical aspects through transdisciplinary approaches, highlighting the critical role of knowledge-driven research in today's academic and industrial landscapes. The series promotes the formation of knowledge-driven communities, particularly in the Information Technology sector, while also bridging diverse fields such as healthcare, education, social sciences, business, and environmental studies to this platform for examining strategies, tools, and best practices that support collaborative and impactful research.

Application of Computational Techniques in Power Systems for Power Quality Improvement
Jagatheesan Kaliannan, Boopathi Dhanasekaran, Sourav Samanta, Anand Baskar, Kanendra Naidu

Knowledge-based Engineering for Innovation
Ketan Sanjay Desale and Soumi Majumder

A Practical Guide to Integrating Generative AI into HR Management
Ketan Sanjay Desale and Soumi Majumder

www.routledge.com/Knowledge-based-Engineering-for-Innovation/book-series/KBEI

A Practical Guide to Integrating Generative AI into HR Management

Ketan Sanjay Desale
Soumi Majumder

CRC Press
Taylor & Francis Group
Boca Raton London New York

CRC Press is an imprint of the
Taylor & Francis Group, an **informa** business
A CHAPMAN & HALL BOOK

Designed cover image: Shutterstock

First edition published 2026
by CRC Press
4 Park Square, Milton Park, Abingdon, Oxon, OX14 4RN

and by CRC Press
2385 NW Executive Center Drive, Suite 320, Boca Raton FL 33431

CRC Press is an imprint of Informa UK Limited

ISBN: 978-1-041-14535-6 (hbk)
ISBN: 978-1-041-14184-6 (pbk)
ISBN: 978-1-003-67488-7 (ebk)

DOI: 10.1201/9781003674887

Typeset in Times
by SPi Technologies India Pvt Ltd (Straive)

Contents

Preface

The fast emergence of generative artificial intelligence (GenAI; generative AI) is transforming each area of business management, and human resources (HR) is among the first to tap into the potential. HR is a growing discipline for all purposes. No longer confined to traditional administrative or support functions, it is becoming more dynamic, data-driven, and strategic. The advent of generative AI enables the automation of complex workflows, personalizing employee experiences, enhancing decision-making, and allowing for unparalleled efficiencies in managing the workforce.

The book on generative AI for HR management evolved from two significant gaps. One is the absence of literature that is both thorough and comprehensible about generative AI use and its implementation in HR. The need for a legal and ethical framework is the second gap addressed by the book. The writing talks about the possibilities and limitations of technology. It suggests that technology can help create job ads and automate candidate screening. Technology can also help with employee engagement, onboarding, and retention. Besides efficiency and innovation, it stresses fairness, transparency, and accountability in AI-enabled HR systems as well.

This book is aimed at HR practitioners, business leaders, policymakers, and AI researchers and is both a roadmap and a reflection. A roadmap toward embedding GenAI into the core HR functions and a reflection on the limits of ethical inclusion. Each of the chapters will help the reader to reimagine HR not as a human versus machines set-up but as a human-empowering ecosystem driven by intelligent technology, through conceptual explanations, real-life case studies, and critical ethical debates.

As generative AI changes the way we work, hire, and grow, this book offers an intellectual foundation to help organizations adopt AI responsibly so that progress is made without compromising dignity, fairness, and trust.

About the Authors

Dr. Ketan Sanjay Desale is a researcher, academician, and technology leader in computer science, with expertise in artificial intelligence, machine learning, and concept drift detection. He holds a Ph.D. in Computer Engineering and has developed a strong academic profile through sustained research contributions and engagement with applied technological innovation.

He currently serves as a Dean IQAC & Associate Professor at ASM's NextGen Technical Campus, Pune, India, where he is involved in teaching, research supervision, and curriculum development. In addition to his academic role, Dr. Desale is responsible for leading digital transformation initiatives at the ASM Group level, focusing on the strategic use of digital technologies to improve institutional processes, information systems, and data-driven decision-making.

Dr. Desale has authored and co-authored numerous research articles published in reputable international journals, including Scopus-indexed publications, and regularly presents his work at national and international conferences. His research contributions span both theoretical and practical dimensions of intelligent systems, reflecting a strong commitment to advancing contemporary computing research.

He actively shares his scholarly work through global research platforms such as Google Scholar, Scopus, and Web of Science, contributing to the broader international scientific community.

Soumi Majumder is a research scholar in the Department of Business and Management at Lincoln University College, Malaysia, and an assistant professor at the Future Business School, Future Institute of Engineering and Management, Kolkata, India. She has more than ten years of academic and two years of industry experience and has previously served at institutions such as Sister Nivedita University, Techno India College of Technology, and NSHM College of Management and Technology. She has authored five books, including titles published by Springer Nature, Taylor & Francis, and Emerald, along with two edited volumes. Her research focuses on quality of work life, stress management, employee engagement, leadership, and entrepreneurship, with more than 25 papers in reputed national and international journals and conferences. She holds one patent and four copyrights from the Government of India and serves as a reviewer for journals by Elsevier, Springer, Emerald, and Sage.

1 Role of Generative AI in HR

Human resource management (HRM) has long focused on people and their hiring, training, motivation, and retention by organizations. In recent months, however, human resource (HR) has been changing as organizations transform and adapt programs and processes to new modes of thinking that accompany rapid growth in technology development. Generative artificial intelligence (GenAI; generative AI), once seen as an emerging technology, could be considered a potentially disruptive technology with the ability to change rapid decision-making, talent management, and organizational growth, which impacts the way HRM works within organizations and across industries.

With technology at one point seen as an area that only supports administrative decisions and back-end systems, technology is now the strategic partner within the HR function and therefore the strategic partner within organizational decision-making, planning, talent management, and growth. Generative AI, with its ability to create, mimic, and personalize content, potentially provides HRM professionals with platforms to improve productivity, products and services; improve processes; increase employee engagement levels; and increase communication.

This chapter investigates the various ways in which generative AI can be used in HRM. We start by explaining what generative AI is and how it has developed over time before discussing how generative AI is different from traditional forms of AI. We will then provide an overview of the HR ecosystem in terms of technology and how HR functions are changing and what challenges and opportunities exist in this new HR landscape. Finally, we discuss how organizations can use generative AI to increase productivity in HR, how to choose the right technologies, and how to ensure data-driven decision-making, with a case study containing the monetary issues of GenAI implementation for small- and medium-sized enterprises (SMEs).

By the end of this chapter, the design for the general AI foundation will provide the reader with a basis for how generative AI can be not only a technological innovation but also strategically a foundation for what we can kickstart, alter, and cultivate as a way to think about transitioning the future of work.

1.1 UNDERSTANDING GENERATIVE AI

Generative AI is an unprecedented advancement in artificial intelligence functionalities, moving from rules-based automation and data analyses to content generation, simulations, and human-like interactions. To appreciate its potential application in HR, we must first understand i) what generative AI is and ii) its origins. In this section, we take a potential definition of generative AI so that we can then spiral back through history, starting with early machine learning models, to classify today's

DOI: 10.1201/9781003674887-1

generative AI platforms that either develop language (textual) or image-based generation (e.g., ChatGPT versus Dall-E). We will also distinguish between generative AI and older functional AI systems that assist organizations, as categorical classification and typology models are very outdated now and why they can provide unique abilities that could fundamentally change HR functions such as recruitment, training, and performance.

1.1.1 Definition: What Is Generative AI?

Generative AI is a type of artificial intelligence model that generates new content—whether text, images, audio, code, or other creative domains—but is similar to, or alludes to, human communication and creativity. The term generative AI includes many types of models and is distinct from traditional AI systems, which are restricted to some form of classification or prediction on the basis of the input alone. Generative AI models extract patterns from a collection of examples and then use those patterns to extract some type of generative output that would be considered original.

Modern generative AI systems usually employ deep learning mechanisms such as generative adversarial networks (GANs) or a family of transformer models (e.g., GPT, BERT, DALL·E). The architecture allows for training models on large datasets, often several terabytes in size, and outputs very realistic content on the basis of the trained dataset while also containing some internal sense of the context within predefined boundaries, depending on the employed framework. This also means that generative AI models function in a way that is not dissimilar to human cognition and meaning, enhancing the value that generative AI affords us in instances where human imitation and reasoning may be primary components of the value equation.

Example applications in HR:

- Autogenerating job descriptions tailored to market trends
- Creating personalized onboarding materials
- Synthesizing employee feedback into actionable summaries

1.1.2 Historical Evolution of Generative AI

Generative AI originated as part of a larger set of advancements in machine learning and artificial intelligence, but its proper functioning, as we see today, has only occurred in the last decade. Table 1.1 illustrates AI in its many forms as we move toward generative AI. AI began in the 1950s–1980s as rule-based systems. The first systems were constrained to narrow domains of logic via symbolic logic and expert systems to perform only the predefined task. At this time, there was no creativity or adaptability, as we have come to expect from computers today, which virtually always operate under a predefined logical working space.

By the 1990s, AI entered the statistical learning period and used algorithms such as support vector machines (SVMs) and decision trees to analyze data via statistical approaches. This is a significant shift away from rule-based reasoning to data-driven predictions using data, but it does not mean that our models were engaging in creativity; there were still only specific classification tasks and optimization tasks

TABLE 1.1
Historical Evolution of GenAI

Year	Milestone	Description
1950s–1980s	Rule-based AI	Early expert systems used logic and rules for decision-making; no generative capabilities.
1990s	Statistical Learning	Algorithms like decision trees and support vector machines began using structured data for predictions.
2014	GANs Introduced	Ian Goodfellow proposed Generative Adversarial Networks, enabling machines to generate realistic images.
2017	Transformers Invented	Google introduced the Transformer architecture, forming the basis for large-scale language models.
2018–2020	Rise of GPT	OpenAI released GPT-2 and GPT-3, capable of generating human-like text from prompts.
2021–2023	Multimodal GenAI	Tools like DALL·E, ChatGPT, and Codex combined text, image, and code generation.
2024+	Enterprise Integration	GenAI began widespread adoption in business operations, including HR, finance, legal, and customer service.

that could use the statistical models. One example of a major breakthrough for AI came in 2014, when Ian Goodfellow and colleagues introduced GANs to generate realistic synthetic images and other data Goodfellow et al. set the stage for the first wave of generative models. In 2017, Google researchers introduced the transformer model architecture, which changed the field of natural language processing (NLP) [1]. This single act would allow for the large-scale creation of large language models capable of generating human-like language.

Between 2018 and 2020, OpenAI released GPT-2 and GPT-3, which demonstrated never-seen-before generative capabilities in producing coherent text that was contextually aware [2]. These advancements made headlines worldwide and demonstrated the practical capabilities of generative models. The years 2021–2023 saw the emergence of multimodal generative AI with models such as DALL·E, Codex, and ChatGPT, which involved generative technology that included text, image, and code generation. These models raised the possibility of cross-domain applications with direct relevance for sectors/industries such as HR, health, and education. Finally, beginning in 2024, we now have enterprise-scale implementations of generative AI. Organizations leverage these technologies in core functions, from HRM to finance and legal services, not only as augmentations for productivity but also as collaborators for creativity or decision-making [3].

This timeline demonstrates the transition of generative AI from theoretical innovation to enterprise use, redefining business activities, including HRM.

Figure 1.1 depicts the key developments in the timeline of generative AI, from rule-based expert systems (1950s–1980s) to statistical learning in the 1990s and full enterprise integration after 2024. Notable milestones include the arrival of GANs in 2014, the release of the transformer in 2017, and the emergence of large generative models such as GPT, DALL·E, and ChatGPT.

FIGURE 1.1 Historical evolution of GenAI.

1.1.3 Traditional AI vs. Generative AI

Understanding the differences between traditional AI and generative AI is needed to understand the revolutionary impact that generative AI has on HRM. Both traditional AI and generative AI are based on machine learning, but they have different intents, outputs, and utility. Traditional AI has been in HRM for decades by providing automation, classifications, and predictions, whereas generative AI is a paradigm shift that enables machines not only to assess data but also to create human-level content, simulate reasoning, and interactively engage in collaboration with HR practitioners.

1.1.3.1 Core Ideas and Problem Framing

Traditional AI models are decision-making models that classify, rank, or predict outcomes. In HRM, this could mean predicting which candidates are most likely to accept an offer or predicting which employees are most likely to quit. In contrast, generative AI models are, by definition, creative. For example, generative AI can generate job descriptions, develop coaching plans, and summarize large volumes of employee commentary into actionable suggestions. In terms of results, traditional AI generally works best when the desired product is a number or category, whereas generative AI performs well when the desired product is usable, with human-readable outputs such as narratives, explanations, or personalized content.

1.1.3.2 Data and Readiness

Further variation involves the variables of the data. Traditional AI relies upon predetermined, structured, labeled datasets to make predictions (e.g., labeled employee performance scores or employee payroll data). For generative AI, data inputs can be structured and unstructured in text and multimodal formats (e.g., policies, handbooks, training program transcripts, and communications).

Essentially, while traditional AI relies on predicting observable patterns among structured datasets, generative AI can make sense of the larger repository of organizational knowledge, regardless of whether it is hidden in documents or siloed in employee email accounts, meaning that generative AI is generally well suited to HR applications in environments where there is a high amount of tacit text-based knowledge.

1.1.3.3 Model Families and Training

Traditional AI encompasses various methods, such as logistic regression, decision trees, random forests, and ensemble models, while using labeled data from an organization to train models. In contrast, generative AI refers generically to models, including but not limited to transformer models, GANs, and diffusion models, which are typically developed through pretraining on enormous corpora of data and then fine-tuning for specific needs or retrieval-augmented generation (RAG) based on secure datasets (e.g., drafting policies or responding to employee questions).

1.1.3.4 Interaction Methods and User Experiences

Traditionally, AI is invisible, producing scores, selections, or rankings on a dashboard showing those scores and automating decisions or actions. Generative AI is a more conversational copilot interaction where HR professionals, managers, and employees can interact with AI through natural language. For example, a manager might use a prompt such as "draft a performance improvement plan according to my company's policy and in language that is supportive." AI will generate a draft, and the human user can accept that draft as is, make edits, and finish.

This transformation changes the HR operating model for users from "request-and-wait" to interactive dialogue, and HR becomes an editor (and approver) to AI drafts rather than creators of the content.

1.1.3.5 Applications Within HR

The distinction in these roles is made clearer in the intended use of both traditional AI and generative AI utilizing HR tasks in Table 1.2. Traditional AI, for example, might predict attrition and assist managers in resume screening or headcount prediction. Generative AI can produce creative, content-heavy tasks such as personalized onboarding guides or interview question sets and training materials or adapt an organization's policy from "HR speak" to a plain-language version for employees.

1.2 EXISTING HR MANAGEMENT SYSTEM

HRM has always been an intricate and multifaceted undertaking requiring a combination of administrative efficiency, strategic intent, and human sensitivity. This section presents an overview of existing HR functions, processes, and organizational models and how they are changing as organizations undergo digital transformation.

TABLE 1.2
Traditional AI vs. Generative AI (Application in HR)

HR Area	Traditional AI (Predict)	Generative AI (Create and Explain)
Talent acquisition	Candidate fit scoring, time-to-fill predictions	Draft job descriptions, create personalized outreach emails, simulate interview responses
Onboarding	Early attrition prediction	Personalized onboarding checklists, policy FAQs, team introductions
Learning and development	Skill-gap detection, recommendation systems	Generate learning paths, summarize course content, create microquizzes
Performance management	Anomaly detection, attrition forecasts	Draft performance review narratives, coaching plans, and development feedback
Policy and compliance	Eligibility checks, exception detection	Policy drafting, plain-language summaries, jurisdiction-specific compliance notes

We look at the questions of how HR departments are changing to accommodate new AI technologies and their associated challenges, including generative AI. Additionally, we discuss some of the challenges organizations face, including data privacy, skill gaps, and denial/change resistance challenges, while looking for new opportunities to enhance personalization, improve talent analytics, and use strategic automation. We provide a roadmap for understanding how HR can move from a reactive service center to a proactive creator of value enabled by AI.

1.2.1 Overview of HR Functions and Processes

HRM entails a plethora of processes related to the management of the employee lifecycle, both as an administrative function (e.g., payroll, compliance) and as a strategic function (talent management, culture). Table 1.3 outlines the core HR functions in organizations today.

While HR systems have largely become computerized systems, many HR systems are still transactional, automating routine processes while incorporating little personalization or creativity. Generative AI will extend these systems even further with the capacity to create dynamic content, simulations, and personalization across these functions.

1.2.2 HR Business Models Under Generative AI

The HR function has evolved dramatically over several decades from a primarily administrative support role to a more strategic business partner [4]. Organizations embraced digitalization and adopted human resource information systems (HRISs) and cloud-based systems to improve sustainability, thus commencing the term digital HR. HR subsequently embarked on predictive analytics, and as a result,

TABLE 1.3
Core HR Functions and Processes

HR Function	Key Processes	Current Technology Use
Recruitment and selection	Job postings, applicant screening, interviews, onboarding	Applicant Tracking Systems (ATS), AI-based resume screening
Training and development	Skills assessment, training programs, career planning	Learning Management Systems (LMS), e-learning platforms
Performance management	Appraisals, feedback, promotions, performance tracking	HR analytics tools, performance dashboards
Compensation and benefits	Payroll, bonuses, health and insurance management	Payroll software, HRIS, compensation benchmarking tools
Employee engagement and retention	Surveys, recognition programs, career growth planning	Employee engagement platforms, digital recognition apps
Compliance and governance	Labor laws, diversity and inclusion, workplace safety	HR compliance management systems, DEI dashboards

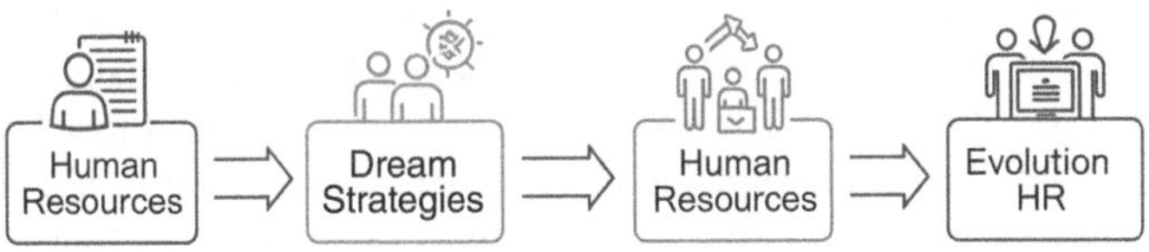

FIGURE 1.2 Evolution of HR business models.

HR departments developed more AI-driven ways of doing business using forecasting tools to inform decision-making in the areas of attrition, workforce planning, and employee engagement.

Today's evolution of generative AI represents the next phase. Generative AI does not simply predict the next word or phrase as in previous models; it actually cocreates HR outputs, dynamically creates policies, can design and personalize onboarding experiences, and dynamically generates pathways for adaptive learning experiences for employees. Generative AI is certainly a copilot for HR professionals, amplifying their efforts and not replacing them. This change through generative AI signals another shift in which transactions become creative and adaptive in aligning closely with creating value for the organization [5].

Figure 1.2 depicts the evolution from transactional HR to a generative AI-based HR function.

This change represents a major shift in how HR is framed in organizations. HR will no longer be framed as a role with only support functions, but in the era of generative AI in HR, it will help organizations reframe HR as an active driver of innovation, organizational culture, and employee empowerment. Hybrid business models that are continuing to emerge in organizations will feature human capabilities and AI systems as complements, whereby HR professionals will be able to leverage actionable insights from AI but continue to exercise their own judgment, empathy, and ethics.

1.2.2.1 Case Study 1.1: Adoption of Generative AI in HR Business Models—Infosys (India)

Infosys, a global leader in IT consulting and IT outsourcing services, demonstrates how generative AI can be implemented in HR business models to produce outcomes. As a company with a workforce of more than 300,000 employees across the globe, Infosys has been utilizing cloud-based HRISs and analytics-based talent management systems for some time. In 2023, they implemented generative AI-powered HR assistants to help with efficiency in recruitment, onboarding, and employee learning.

- **Recruitment**: AI-generated job descriptions ensure inclusivity and alignment with diverse goals, reducing bias in hiring communications.
- **Onboarding**: AI-driven chatbots deliver personalized learning modules, FAQs, and policy guidance to new hires, easing HR administrative loads.
- **Learning and Development**: Adaptive content creation allows the design of career pathways tailored to employees' skills and aspirations.

The results were significant. Infosys demonstrated a 30% reduction in time-to-hire and a 25% increase in onboarding experience scores [6]. Additionally, HR employees moved from administrative functions and were better able to focus on strategic initiatives such as leadership pipeline development and cultural fit alignment. This example illustrates how generative AI can deliver value to HR by transforming HR from a tactical support function to a strategic copilot and changing business models from personalization, innovation, and human–machine teaming.

1.2.3 Challenges in New HR Management

Despite the many significant advantages, the implementation of AI, particularly generative AI for HR management, presents many challenges. Foremost among these issues are the data privacy and data security risks involved. HR systems often store very sensitive and confidential employee data, for example, personal data, performance records, financial data, etc. Generative tools increase the likelihood of data misuse or data leakage and associated legal liabilities under strict regimes such as the General Data Protection Regulation (GDPR) in Europe and India's Digital Personal Data Protection Act [7]. Therefore, if an organization decides to use AI, secure deployment and strong access control should be the first priority before implementing AI. The next challenge concerns fairness and bias.

Traditional AI systems have already been accused of being biased in-built, such as Amazon's shelved AI hiring tool, which unfairly penalized women job applicants [8]. When left unchecked, generative AI can perpetuate and even amplify such biases in recruitment ads, policy documents, or performance evaluations. This escalates the risk of discriminatory practices being ingrained in HR automation, defeating the purpose of building inclusive workplaces. Resistance to change is also a major hindrance. Employees and HR professionals can be resistant to or apprehensive about AI adoption, anticipate job loss, or fail to believe in machine-suggested ideas. Such resistance to change can prevent adoption and slow organizational change, particularly with poor communication and training [9].

In addition, artificial intelligence highlights significant gaps in the technical competencies of HR departments. Most professionals within this field are not well equipped with the technical expertise necessary for effectively assessing, verifying, or regulating AI systems, resulting in high dependency on third-party vendors or experts. Such dependency can lead to a threat to long-term sustainability and diminished organizational control over AI-informed HR practices. Finally, legal and ethical considerations represent an extensive challenge. AI applications for monitoring worker behavior, assessing performance, or surveillance in the workplace present significant questions of autonomy, dignity, and transparency [10]. Unregulated application can undermine employee confidence and put organizations at risk of reputational damage that does not strike a balance between efficiency and ethical demands.

Together, these issues point toward developing responsible AI HR practices—based on transparency, fairness, privacy, and human agency—to make the adoption of generative AI enhance organizational trustworthiness and inclusivity rather than erode them. Surveillance gives rise to ethical issues of autonomy, dignity, and transparency [10].

1.2.4 Opportunities for the Adoption of AI Technology

While integrating generative AI into HR comes with challenges, it also presents unprecedented opportunities to be more efficient, innovative, and employee-centric. One of the greatest opportunities is the personalization of HR processes. Traditional digital HR systems deliver standardized experiences, and generative tools can tailor onboarding programs, career development paths, and training materials to individual employees. This personalization can lead to increased engagement, satisfaction, and retention, as employees feel more valued and supported in their careers. Generative AI also enables content creation at scale, which is highly relevant in HR functions that involve much documentation and communication. From drafting inclusive job descriptions and updating policy manuals to generating localized compliance reports and training content, AI can produce high-quality output at scale and in multiple formats. This reduces the administrative burden on HR professionals and ensures consistency and speed in internal comms.

Another opportunity is better decision-making within HR departments. Predictive analytics has already allowed organizations to forecast attrition rates, identify high potential employees, and optimize workforce planning. Generative AI builds on these capabilities by providing contextualized narratives and scenario simulations. For example, instead of just predicting attrition, AI could generate tailored recommendations on intervention strategies, providing HR managers with foresight and actionable insights. Generative AI also supports employee self-service and empowerment. Conversational AI and chatbots can provide real-time, 24/7 answers to employee queries on benefits, leave policies, payroll, or compliance. These tools reduce the workload on HR staff while simultaneously providing employees with immediate access to accurate information so that they can feel more transparent and responsive. Finally, the adoption of generative AI can drive strategic change in HR's role within the organization. By automating mundane and repetitive tasks, HR professionals can focus on higher-value activities such as shaping culture, developing leadership pipelines, and aligning human capital strategies with business objectives. In this way, generative AI is a strategic partner, not just an efficiency tool, and HR's evolving role as a value creator [5]. Overall, these opportunities mean that generative AI can be a transformative enabler in HR, not only in terms of being more efficient but also in terms of how we engage, develop, and retain our workforce. With good governance and thoughtful implementation, AI can elevate HR into a more adaptive, creative, and strategic function that is fit for the fast-changing world of work.

Table 1.4 illustrates the dual nature of generative AI in HR. On the left, key challenges such as privacy risks, bias, and skill gaps highlight potential barriers to adoption. On the right, opportunities such as personalization, decision-making support, and strategic transformation demonstrate the technology's potential as an enabler of HR innovation.

TABLE 1.4
Challenges and Opportunities of Generative AI in HR

Challenges in New HR Management	Opportunities for AI Adoption
Data privacy and security risks (GDPR, DPDP)	Personalized HR processes (onboarding, learning paths)
Bias and fairness issues in recruitment and evaluation	Scalable content creation (policies, training, job posts)
Resistance to change from employees and HR staff	Improved decision-making with predictive + generative insights
Skill gaps in AI literacy within HR departments	Employee self-service and empowerment through AI chatbots
Ethical and legal concerns in surveillance and monitoring	Strategic transformation of HR's role toward value creation

1.3 INCREASING HR PRODUCTIVITY WITH GENERATIVE AI

Generative AI presents an opportunity to increase HR productivity, as departments look to become more agile and operate efficiently in a challenging environment. In this chapter, we look at the applications of generative AI in recruitment, onboarding, employee communication, policy creation, and learning and development to show how it can be seamlessly embedded in these processes. We examine how the right tools can be identified, the technologies properly chosen, and the workflows crafted to yield the most Return on Investment (ROI) while still respecting organizational objectives. To highlight these lessons, we use a case study that analyzes the financial and operational effects of adopting generative AI in SMEs to provide a guide for scalable usage.

1.3.1 Understanding Generative AI and Its Applications in HR

Generative AI is a system that is capable of creating human-like content—text, images, and synthetic datasets—on the basis of large-scale learning from source information [11]. In HR, this applies in real-world scenarios throughout the employee lifecycle:

- **Hiring and Talent Acquisition**: AI can design job postings that eliminate bias, compose interview questions, and serve up lists of candidates by specific skills.
- **Onboarding and Training**: Generative models can create customized new employee manuals, training materials, and policy summaries on the basis of a new employee's job and location.
- **Employee Communication**: AI assistants and bots enable communication by answering routine questions, helping employees with HR-related work, and providing support in several languages.

- **Performance Management**: AI-generated dashboards and reports offer managers performance information, which remains transparent and minimizes evaluation bias.
- **Knowledge Management**: Generative AI can transform existing HR documents (e.g., benefits policies and compliance guides) into usable formats such as FAQs, video scripts, or employee handbooks.
- By integrating day-to-day work with AI, HR professionals have more time for high-impact initiatives, and employees receive better access and quicker responses from HR systems.

1.3.2 Choosing the Right Tools and Technologies

Selecting the appropriate generative AI (GenAI) tools is absolutely critical for organizations to gain from AI developments in HR management. While GenAI presents great potential, success depends on pairing it with what the organization requires, its existing systems, and compliance needs. HR leaders need to use a clear plan that makes the tools work well today and that will also be lasting and ethical. The functional fit is the first key aspect. GenAI tools need to address the top HR issues of an organization. For example, firms facing hiring challenges may prioritize AI tools for hiring that can sift resumes, generate equitable job descriptions, or interlink candidates with jobs on the basis of their skills. Similarly, companies looking to build their workforce might employ AI-driven learning management systems (LMSs) that create learning content that adjusts to how workers work. The idea is not to use AI for amusement but rather to make the tools selected accomplish significant HR objectives such as quicker hiring, improved employee retention, or increased learning engagement.

The second is scalability and integration. HR processes are very rarely operational in isolation; they depend greatly on integrated systems such as HRISs, payroll management, and enterprise resource planning (ERP). A generative AI solution that operates as a pilot in isolation might not be able to deliver long-term value if it does not scale or integrate with large systems. For example, integrating GenAI into products such as SAP SuccessFactors or Workday enables organizations to scale incrementally, delivering AI-powered recruitment, onboarding, or performance management capabilities without impacting core operations. Therefore, HR leaders should focus not only on short-term advantages but also on the tool's potential to scale with the growth of the organization.

The third dimension is related to governance and compliance, which is an increasingly salient issue given the regulatory environment around AI and data use. Generative AI tools must adhere to local and international data privacy regulations such as the GDPR in Europe or the Digital Personal Data Protection Act (DPDP, 2023) in India. Adherence to internal governance frameworks is also essential and provides a protocol to reduce the risk of bias, discrimination, and abuse, such as in promotions, compensation, or performance reviews, at times when HR sensitivity is paramount. Further ethical AI usage calls for transparency and explainability to ensure that HR and employees understand the basis of decisions made and the role that AI plays in that decision-making process [12].

These issues are highlighted in Table 1.5 as a decision-making framework for HR leaders to consider in their use of GenAI tools. By considering both functional fit and scalability alongside governance, organizations can take advantage of the opportunities presented by technology that improve efficiency but also meet the organization's lawful objectives of accountability and fairness.

The successful integration of generative AI into HR is based on the careful consideration of three interrelated areas, as shown in Figure 1.3. Functional fit means that the generative AI tools selected meet the organization's current HR requirements, whether they are recruiting, employee engagement, learning and development, etc. Scalability and integration means that the tools can integrate with current HRIS and enterprise systems and can be scaled in the future without creating

TABLE 1.5
Framework for Selecting Generative AI Tools in HR

Criteria	Key Considerations	Examples
Functional fit	Recruitment, onboarding, L&D, performance management	LinkedIn Talent Insights, Eightfold
Scalability and integration	Compatibility with HRIS, adaptability to future AI modules	SAP SuccessFactors + GenAI APIs
Governance and compliance	Bias mitigation, explainability, GDPR/DPDP alignment, data security	Microsoft Viva with AI, OpenAI HR APIs

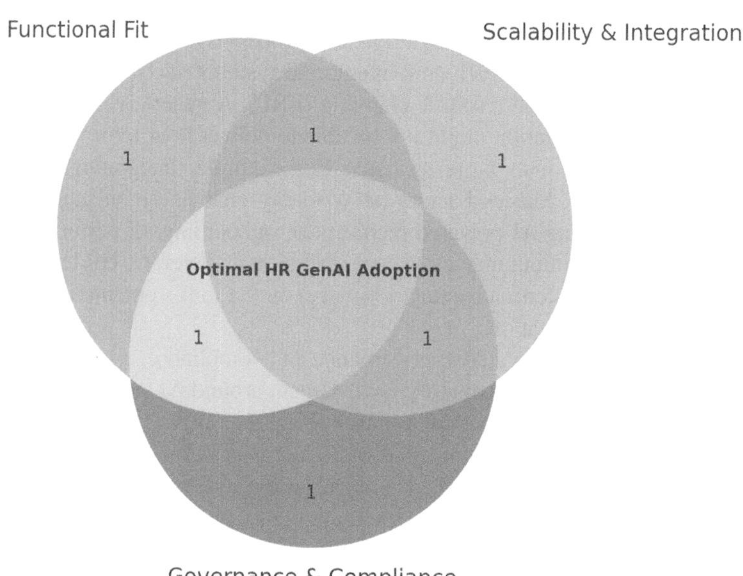

FIGURE 1.3 Intersection of key criteria for selecting GenAI tools in HR.

operational interruptions. Governance and compliance stave off ethical risks, regulatory infractions, and the potential for bias or opacity in HR decision-making. It is within the intersection of these three areas that the "Optimal HR GenAI Adoption Zone" appears, giving organizations operational and financial advantages but also a responsible pathway for AI-enabled transformation in HR practices that is future-proof.

1.3.3 Case Study: Financial Implications of GenAI Adoption for SMEs

SMEs constitute more than 90% of enterprises globally and represent an important source of employment and economic growth. However, many SMEs face particular challenges in HR management, including limited resources, small HR staff, and greater employee turnover. The following case study describes how the adoption of generative AI could address these challenges and generate tangible returns on investment.

- **Background**: A mid-sized manufacturer located in Pune, India (2024), with 850 employees, faced increasing administrative bottlenecks in its HR department. The firm had only six HR staff members, and they struggled to perform the repetitive tasks associated with answering employee inquiries (e.g., leave policy clarifications, errors related to payroll, requesting dates for training, etc.) and initiating drafting job descriptions for recruiting, creating documents to satisfy compliance requirements, etc. Internal surveys also indicated low employee satisfaction with HR response times—often employees waited 2–3 working days to receive responses to simple queries.
- **Implementation**: To eliminate these inefficiencies in HR tasks, the firm used a subscription-based generative AI-powered HR chatbot as part of its existing HRIS. The organization's chatbot was operated by training it on the organization's documents (policy manuals, payroll residency guidelines, training documents, etc.) and deploying it as a multilingual chatbot (English, Hindi, Marathi) with text-to-speech capability to support the firm's multilingual workforce.

The implementation was deployed in two phases:

- The pilot phase (three months in duration) focused on responding to common HR questions.
- The expansion phase (six months in duration) included the automation of job description writing and first-level employee responses to performance evaluation comments.

There were positive outcomes as a result of GenAI adoption by HR, which indicated relatively measurable advantages such as the following:

- **Time Savings**: HR staff reportedly spent approximately 25 hours each week answering common inquiries. When the evolution to the chatbot occurred, the time spent dropped to 5 hours/week in common inquiry responses. A reduction of 20 hours/week (1,000 hours or 120 days/year) would mean that HR staff have opportunities to engage in more value-added HR work, such as employee engagement and succession planning.

- **Cost Savings**: The organization calculated cost savings at an average HR staff cost of INR 1,800/hour and used this to calculate possible HR cost savings of INR 18 lakhs (USD 22,000) annually spent responding to common inquiries.
- **Productivity Gains**: Employees reported 70% better response time when the chatbot was used to answer common inquiries, with most employee questions being answered instantaneously by the time the employee initiated the chatbot for their inquiry. Satisfaction surveys also indicated marked improvements, with HR service quality ratings improving by 40% in six months.
- **Scalability**: Perhaps one of the most important advantages was the only additional minor investment (approximately INR 4 lakhs for software subscription and onboarding), thus indicating that the adaptation of HR processes, such as AI-assisted recruitment screening, could be sustained for future use.

The case illustrates how, for SMEs where the optimization of resources is crucial, adopting modular AI (through subscription services instead of more traditional infrastructure investments) can generate substantial returns on investment. The deployment also illustrated that generative AI can quickly render SME HR functions more effective, "punching above their weight," and improve service quality in HR as they strive to be more like larger companies and "bring them into line" with the service levels of larger companies.

The case study highlighted numerous lessons for SMEs when considering adopting generative AI in HR. First, the phased approach proved to be very effective in reducing risk. Starting small with simple query handling and moving into the more complex recruitment and performance management domains allowed the organization to trial the technology, change the workflows, and build trust with employees without major dislocation. Second, the outcomes pointed toward the opportunity for human–AI interaction [13]. Generative AI is not about replacing HR staff; it is about augmenting their roles. The staff automates repetitive tasks, allowing HR specialists to redirect their efforts toward higher-value activities such as employee engagement, succession planning, and training strategies. This collaborative model retains human oversight while also improving the output of HR services. Finally, the financial viability of the monthly subscription-based generative AI tools proved to be a key enabler for SMEs to adopt them. Small businesses work with leaner resources than larger firms with large technology budgets do. The subscription model allows the organization to access leading-edge AI solutions while avoiding expensive infrastructure costs, making adoption as affordable and scalable as possible. Collectively, these takeaways illustrate how generative AI can provide strategic and financial value to SMEs when they are considering adoption intentionally and progressively.

As presented in Figure 1.4, generative AI aided the HR function in achieving notable improvements in efficiency, cost, and employee experience. The HR time

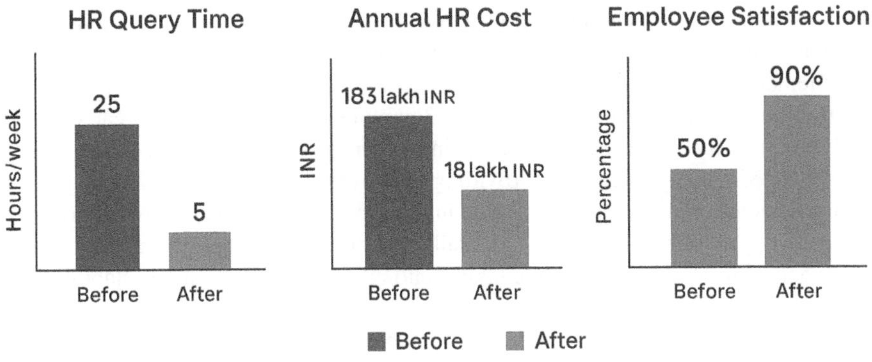

FIGURE 1.4 Cost–benefit analysis of GenAI adoption in an SME HR system.

spent on queries decreased from 25 to 5 hours a week, highlighting the productivity implications of automating routine, low-value work. These efficiencies then manifest in actual financial savings as annual HR costs decreased from INR 36 to 18 lakhs, supporting the case for subscription-based AI adoption for SMEs. More importantly, employee satisfaction increased from 50% to 90% in the six months following the implementation of generative AI in HR. The increase can be linked to faster response times, accessibility to HR services, and the ability of HR staff to shift toward more personal employee engagement. Taken together, these results underscore the financial and strategic advantages of GenAI adoption in SMEs, particularly when it is applied to routine yet resource-intensive HR processes.

This chapter offers a synthesis of the indispensable position of generative AI in digitizing HRM. Section 1.1 introduces definitions of generative AI and a historical perspective that moves from symbolic systems through machine learning to large language models (LLMs). Importantly, the component of generative AI that differentiates it from traditional AI is inferential decision-making, which is subject to function but where the user introduces a range of contextual conditions that could sensibly influence decision-making. Therefore, traditional AI represents an imperative form of deterministic, rule-based artificial intelligence, whereas generative AI introduces a dynamic, creative, and adaptive decision-making facilitator in a user-generated context. This infuses a dimension of reliability in HR study and practice into real-world decision-making irrespective of an AI solution.

In Section 1.2, we explored the notion of the current HR management system, depicting some of the functions and processes of HRM (recruitment and hiring, onboarding, learning and development, performance evaluation, and employee engagement), which can provide a digitized dynamic HRM framework for an organizational strategy. Furthermore, the shift of HR business models toward generative AI and their function and traditional innovation with operational efficiency now operates at slightly different levels, generating strategies, analytics, and decision frameworks with all the power of automation. The reward space for AI adoption that was identified and explored represents a significant opportunity, from automating functions to governance and predictive analytics. Unsurprisingly, the risks associated with rewards were highlighted and included challenges with integration within legacy systems, ethical issues such as bias, and frontline and back-end data governance requirements.

Building on this foundation, Section 1.3 explores how generative AI can enhance HR productivity in practice. Specific implementations such as AI-based hiring, personalized employee training, providing employee support through virtual conversational agents, and predictive analytics in workforce management were discussed as primary opportunities for impact. Equally important, the importance of selecting tools and technology wisely while taking into account functionality, scalability, and governance was also discussed.

With the subsequent real-world case study presented by an SME, the financial and strategic realities of GenAI implementation were highlighted: the associated HR costs were reduced, the query resolution time was faster, employee satisfaction improved, and the tangible financial payoff of implementing GenAI in practice.

The documentation of these realities demonstrates that generative AI is no longer a pie-in-the-sky innovative technology; rather, it is a practical technology to transform HR, but these benefits may be realized only if the technology is implemented intentionally, ethically, and strategically aligned with organizational goals. In summary, generative AI provides both SMEs and larger companies the opportunity to transform HR from a support function to a key enabler of organizational resilience, performance, and growth. The following chapters set the agenda for further discussions on the adoption of generative AI in HR by discussing ethics, governance frameworks, and sector-based applications of generative AI in human capital management.

REFERENCES

1. Vaswani, A., Shazeer, N., Parmar, N., Uszkoreit, J., Jones, L., . . ., Polosukhin, I. (2017). Attention is all you need. *31st Conference on Neural Information Processing Systems (NeurIPS 2017)*, Long Beach, CA.
2. Brown, T., Mann, B., Ryder, N., Subbiah, M., Kaplan, J., . . ., Amodei, D. (2020). Language models are few-shot learners. *34th Conference on Neural Information Processing Systems (NeurIPS 2020)*, Vancouver, Canada.
3. Gartner (2024). *Generative AI in business operations: Strategic integration report.*
4. Ulrich, D. (1997). *Human Resource Champions: The Next Agenda for Adding Value and Delivering Results*. Harvard Business Press.
5. Boudreau, J. W., & Cascio, W. F. (2017). Human capital analytics: Why are we not there? *Journal of Organizational Effectiveness: People and Performance*, 4(2).
6. Infosys. (2023). Infosys Annual Report 2023: Building tomorrow's enterprise with AI. Infosys Ltd. Retrieved from https://www.infosys.com
7. Voigt, P., & Von dem Bussche, A. (2017). *The EU General Data Protection Regulation (GDPR)*. Springer.
8. Dastin, J. (2018). *Amazon Scraps Secret AI Recruiting Tool That Showed Bias Against Women*. Reuters.
9. Tursunbayeva, A., Di Lauro, S., & Pagliari, C. (2018). People analytics—A scoping review of conceptual boundaries and value propositions. *International Journal of Information Management*, 43, 224–247.

10. Ball, K. (2021). Workplace surveillance: An overview. *New Technology, Work and Employment*, 36(1), 1–19.
11. Bommasani, R., Hudson, D. A., Adeli, E., Altman, R., Arora, S., von Arx, S., . . . & Liang, P. (2021). *On the Opportunities and Risks of Foundation Models*. Stanford University, Center for Research on Foundation Models.
12. Majumder, S., & Dey, N. (2022). Artificial intelligence and knowledge management. In Janusz Kacprzyk ed., *AI-empowered Knowledge Management* (pp. 85–100). Springer Singapore.
13. Majumder, S., & Dey, N. (2023). Artificial intelligence: The future of people management. In Jagdish Chand Bansal, Joong Hoon Kim, Atulya K. Nagar, eds., *The Vogue of Managing People in Workplace* (pp. 83–102). Springer Nature Singapore.

2 GenAI Transforming HR

The integration of generative artificial intelligence (GenAI; generative AI) into the space of human resources (HR) rewrites the management of employees, revolutionizing old traditional processes while unlocking innovative opportunities within them. From recruiting and engaging employees to talent development strategies and retention, GenAI is not just a tool but also a transformative force that drives unprecedented efficiency, personalization, and strategic insight.

At the heart of this is the ability of GenAI to generate human-like text, simulate conversations, and analyze vast datasets with high precision. This allows the automation of mundane tasks for HR professionals, the provision of personalized solutions, and increased data-driven decision-making capabilities with greater confidence. The new AI-powered chatbots are now able to address most routine employee inquiries, while algorithms are sophisticated enough to draft job descriptions and screen candidates to free up valuable time and resources.

However, this paradigm shift creates a host of ethical, legal, and operational concerns that organizations must navigate. Issues such as bias in the outputs produced by AI, data privacy, and potential dehumanization of HR processes highlight the need for careful design, implementation, and governance of generative AI tools. As HR moves from a transactional to a more strategic position, practitioners must balance the use of AI capabilities with the need to preserve the human-focused nature of their profession.

This chapter takes an in-depth look at how GenAI affects HR and its potential benefits and challenges. On the basis of practical applications and ethical issues, we explore in greater detail how GenAI is changing HR and redefining the future of work.

2.1 GENAI IMPACT ON HR

Generative AI has profoundly changed the operational dynamics of HR, enabling the formation of more intelligent, swift, and customized solutions. This chapter delves into the groundbreaking capabilities of GenAI in essential areas of HR management while focusing on its impact and provides references to academic articles for further research.

2.1.1 Automation of Routine HR Functions

The cyclical nature of routine HR activities often prevents the department from focusing on strategic initiatives that help in the development of the organization. Activities such as answering employee queries, scheduling interviews, processing payroll, and managing employee documentation are basic but time-consuming. Generative AI is changing this landscape by offering sophisticated automation solutions that can increase efficiency while ensuring consistency and scalability in HR operations.

DOI: 10.1201/9781003674887-2

2.1.1.1 AI-Powered Chatbots

GenAI-powered chatbots are among the most widely used applications in HR automation. They can be designed to respond to a vast range of employee queries from company policies and leave entitlements to even complex processes such as onboarding and benefit enrollment.

- **Enhanced Accessibility**: These chatbots are always available and ready to help employees with immediate support irrespective of the time zone or office hours.
- **Scalability**: They can handle interactions with hundreds of employees at the same time, thereby reducing wait times.
- **Continuous Learning**: Many of these tools use machine learning to improve over time, thereby ensuring that responses remain relevant and precise.

Studies reveal that such tools increasingly influence HR. For example, AI-driven chatbots reduce resolution times by 50% for employee queries while increasing overall satisfaction rates.

2.1.1.2 Document Automation

In addition to the conversational interface, GenAI is revolutionizing how HR performs documentation. Starting from contract drafting to producing performance appraisal reports, GenAI systems minimize human interference in manual and repetitive documentation processes.

- **Error Reduction**: Automation reduces the likelihood of human error, especially when sensitive documents such as employee contracts and compliance reports are used.
- **Speed and Efficiency**: Tasks that used to require hours or days, for example, writing detailed job descriptions, can now be done in minutes.
- **Customization at Scale**: GenAI enables HR teams to create personalized documents tailored to individual roles, departments, or needs, enhancing communication clarity and employee trust.

For example, tools such as DocuAI have been proven to accelerate HR document workflows by 70% while ensuring compliance with organizational and legal standards.

2.1.1.3 Benefits for HR Professionals

The automation of routine activities does more than save the time of HR professionals by allowing them to focus their efforts on higher-value activities such as developing employee engagement, leadership, and strategic workforce planning.

A study [1] has shown that organizations embracing AI-driven HR automation experience a 30% reduction in administrative burdens. This empowers HR teams to better utilize resources in activities directly contributing to organizational success.

2.1.1.4 Case Studies

2.1.1.4.1 Case Study: IBM's Use of AI in HR

This case from IBM shows how AI will revolutionized processes in its organization by facilitating smooth changes in processes and enhancing effectiveness. The company leveraged its AI platform, Watson, to automate repetitive HR activities, including handling employee questions, creating offer letters, and monitoring performance reviews. Such automation resulted in efficiency in operations as well as a considerable improvement in employee satisfaction; the handling of queries significantly decreased from days to seconds, indicating faster issue resolution. The company also reported a 20% growth in employee satisfaction scores on the basis of the improved responsiveness and accuracy of AI-powered interactions. The system's near-zero error rate in producing more than 500,000 documents annually further solidifies its reliability and scalability. IBM's success story is a testament to how AI can optimize HR workflows and foster a more satisfied and engaged workforce.

- Source: IBM Official AI and HR Transformation Report, 2020.

2.1.1.4.2 Case Study: Unilever Recruitment Automation

Unilever's adoption of AI for recruitment demonstrates how automation can revolutionize hiring processes. By integrating chatbots and AI-powered tools, Unilever streamlined candidate screening and interview scheduling, significantly enhancing efficiency and the user experience. This approach led to a remarkable 75% reduction in time-to-hire, enabling the company to fill positions more quickly and effectively. Automated scheduling tools relieved recruiters from laborious administrative work, enabling them to gain 40% of their time to work on strategic and personalization activities. In addition, this streamlined and transparent process meant that candidates' experiences improved; indeed, 90% of the applicants were satisfied. The story of Unilever reveals how AI can strike the right balance between operational efficiency and positive engagement with the candidate.

- Source: Harvard Business Review, *AI-Powered Recruitment at Unilever* (2021).

2.1.1.4.3 Case Study: Accenture AI-Powered Chatbots for Employee Support

Accenture is a prime example of an organization that has utilized AI-powered chatbots to deliver HR support to its employees. In such a large organization, Accenture has more than 500,000 employees and rolled out AI-driven chatbots to cater to most HR-related queries. The system is very effective and reduces the workload of the HR support team by 40%, answering more than 1.2 million queries per year. In addition, the rollout reduced employee resolution times from an average of 48 hours to a minute or less, leading to faster and more responsive support. This case history demonstrates how AI can unlock operational scalability, reduce friction, and dramatically improve the satisfaction of employees through expedited service delivery.

- Source: Accenture AI in HR Transformation Insights (2022).

2.1.1.5 Challenges and Considerations

Although automation provides various benefits, implementing automation is not without hurdles:

- **Data Privacy and Security**: Automated systems often handle sensitive employee data, necessitating robust security measures to prevent breaches.
- **Change Management**: Organizations must manage resistance from employees and ensure that the HR staff is adequately trained to effectively use these tools.
- **Ethical Concerns**: AI must be transparent so that the system does not favor anyone and that employees are treated equally.

By addressing these challenges, organizations can fully harness the transformative potential of GenAI in automating routine HR functions, creating a more agile and productive workforce.

2.1.2 Personalized Delivery of HR Services

Personalization has emerged as a foundation for employee satisfaction and engagement. Organizations are increasingly leveraging generative AI (GenAI) to deliver more tailored HR services. This allows HR teams to tailor services to the needs of each employee by considering their preferences, skills, and professional aspirations.

- **Learning and Development**: AI-powered tools bridge skill gaps by analyzing employee performance data and recommending personalized training programs. For example, AI can pinpoint specific areas for improvement and curate learning paths that align with individual career goals, such as video tutorials, interactive courses, or real-world projects. This targeted approach not only accelerates professional growth but also increases motivation and retention. Studies such as [2] demonstrate a 25% increase in employee engagement if personalized learning modules are implemented effectively, thus indicating the influence of personalization on workforce development.
- **Customized Onboarding**: Tailored onboarding is another space where AI truly thrives. Standardized onboarding materials often confuse new hires since they are too general to cover role-specific needs. GenAI analyzes job descriptions and departmental requirements to create customized onboarding guides, virtual mentors, and task-specific training for new employees. Personalized onboarding experiences enhance productivity and minimize time-to-value. Research findings show that employees who have role-focused onboarding are more likely to be confident and capable in the early days of their time in the organization, which helps to ensure long-term satisfaction and performance.

This research continues to grow and highlights the pivotal role that AI plays in HR personalization. For instance, [2] highlights the crucial relationship between AI-technology-based personalization and rising engagement, especially in areas of onboarding and learning. Similarly, a report by Deloitte underlines that an overwhelming 83% of organizations implementing personalized HR services have witnessed significant development in terms of employee satisfaction and organizational loyalty. Integrating GenAI into HR processes helps organizations establish a culture of continuous development and support. This allows employees to be valued and understood at each point in their journey. This ensures not only individual performance but also organizational success in this competitive landscape of talent.

2.1.3 Data-Driven Talent Ecosystem

Generative AI transforms human resource management (HRM) into an analytics-oriented department, meaning that more evidence-based talent acquisition decisions have a good foundation, resulting in ideal performance analysis and more effective workforce planning. Thus, it streamlines the work so that organizations can gain optimized insights regarding their employees to attain strategic business orientation by achieving better flexibility under rapidly shifting business directions and visions.

2.1.3.1 Predictive Analytics for Proactive Decision-Making

GenAI allows HR departments to track workforce trends and make informed decisions on the basis of predictive analytics. AI models analyze enormous databases of historical and real-time data to assess the likelihood of employee attrition risk and predict skill gaps and future talent needs. For example, algorithms would be able to pick trends in engagement, workload, and feedback data to pinpoint specific employees at risk of walking out. Following such assessments, proactive retention strategies could include a personalized development program or an adjustment in the role to combat turnover.

Predictive analytics also helps in workforce planning by predicting the skills crucial for future business growth. According to a McKinsey study in organizations that use AI-based predictive technology, the ability to identify proactive skill shortages increased by 30%. This information empowers HR teams to plan selective upskilling and selective recruitment to ensure that the right employees are in place to face future challenges.

2.1.3.2 AI-Powered Candidate Screening

This is the most resource-intensive phase of the recruitment process and has been redefined with the advent of GenAI. With the analysis of hundreds and thousands of resumes, application forms, and candidate profiles, AI tools identify the best candidates on the basis of objective parameters such as qualifications, experience, and skills. The advanced Natural Language Processing (NLP) capabilities of AI tools ensure that nuanced information, such as cultural fit or soft skills, is analyzed through interview responses or written assessments.

GenAI crucially reduces unconscious bias in hiring by standardizing the criteria for evaluation. A study by [3] showed that, compared with traditional methods, AI-based screening of candidates reduced errors on the basis of bias by 35%. In this way, the hiring process becomes faster, and a diverse workforce is created.

2.1.3.3 Real-Time Performance Insights

GenAI is what leads performance evaluation toward continuous monitoring and data analysis instead of periodic assessments. AI tracks Key Performance Indicators (KPIs), contributions to projects, and feedback in the real world, providing a holistic perspective on overall performance. Continuous monitoring facilitates the timely identification of high performers for leadership purposes and can also be corrected at points of underperformance.

For example, GenAI can create custom performance dashboards that provide visual representations of employee strengths, accomplishments, and areas for development, thus ensuring more effective feedback sessions. Additionally, AI-based insights enable managers to customize recognition and development plans according to individual needs, which enhances engagement and productivity. According to a report from Gartner [4], firms that utilized AI for performance management witnessed a 25% rise in employee satisfaction and a 20% decline in turnover rates.

The study by [5] focused on the transformative effect of data analytics in HRM, with a specific focus on how AI-driven talent analytics improve the hiring quality and retention of employees. By using data from organizations operating in different industries, the research highlights how AI enables HR teams to make informed, data-driven decisions at all stages of the talent lifecycle. One of the main takeaways is that adding AI-based analytics tools to the recruitment process improves the quality of hires by 20%. This is accomplished through AI models evaluating large datasets such as resumes, application materials, and performance indicators to select the right candidates on the basis of objective criteria such as skill alignment and cultural fit. This helps eliminate biases when evaluating candidates and, hence, results in more diversified and inclusive hiring outcomes.

In terms of retention, the study revealed that AI's ability to analyze employee sentiment, engagement patterns, and performance metrics allows organizations to proactively identify at-risk employees and implement tailored retention strategies. This capability led to a 20% improvement in retention rates among companies using AI-driven analytics. Examples of successful strategies include personalized development plans, targeted employee recognition programs, and adjustments to workloads on the basis of individual preferences and capacities.

2.1.4 Enhanced Productivity and Candidate Experience

Generative AI has emerged as a potent tool for organizations seeking optimal recruitment processes and increased employee productivity. GenAI streamlines administrative tasks and enables highly dynamic, personalized interactions by improving the operational efficiency of HR teams while enhancing the experience of candidates and employees.

2.1.4.1 Smart Recruitment Platforms

Recruitment platforms powered by AI redefine the manner in which organizations interact with prospective hires. These platforms are designed to use GenAI, which enables dynamic, two-way communication with applicants to share real-time updates and offer them specific job recommendations and immediate feedback. For example, it can answer frequently asked questions, guide candidates in the application process, and schedule interviews autonomously. This automation not only enhances candidate engagement but also reduces the burden on HR teams, allowing them to focus on more strategic aspects of hiring.

Real-time feedback and transparency in recruitment create a positive candidate experience. Candidates feel valued and informed throughout the process, improving the employer's brand perception. According to LinkedIn Talent Solutions (2022), 83% of candidates reported that receiving timely updates and personalized feedback significantly improved their opinion of the hiring company. Furthermore, AI tools reduce the average time-to-hire by 60%, as highlighted by [6] Deloitte's Future of Work report (2023), ensuring that organizations can secure top talent more efficiently.

2.1.4.2 Employee Productivity Tools

Beyond recruitment, GenAI-based platforms increase employee productivity by monitoring workload, identifying bottlenecks, and recommending tailored solutions to improve work performance. Such platforms utilize real-time data from different sources of information, including a range of project management, communications, and feedback sites, toward actionable insights. For example, AI easily identifies patterns of overloaded work or inefficiencies, provides suggestions for job redistribution, automates repetitive activities, and schedules focused time for essential projects.

Moreover, AI-based systems enable personalized goal setting and professional development through the analysis of individual performance data. For example, employees can be suggested skill-building opportunities that are aligned with their career aspirations. According to PwC (2021), companies that implemented AI-based productivity tools experienced a 20% increase in workforce efficiency and a 15% decrease in burnout rates because of better workload management.

2.1.4.3 Candidate-Centric Recruitment Experience

GenAI improves the recruitment process by making it more inclusive and personalized. NLP- and sentiment analysis-based tools ensure that communication is individual-specific and is based on the candidate's preferences and career goals. With virtual interview assistants, now powered by GenAI, candidates gain insights into the role, company culture, and expectations, preparing them for the hiring process.

HireVue, through its case study published in 2022, reported a 30% jump in candidate satisfaction scores through the integration of AI-driven recruitment tools. The improved results can be attributed to the more human-like personalized touch in the AI interaction with candidates. Therefore, such systems create a smooth and streamlined application process, leading applicants to conclude the process by lowering drop-out rates.

The study by [7] discussed the deep impact of AI on modern recruitment practices, specifically how AI-based platforms enhance operational efficiency and candidate satisfaction. Through data analysis of organizations that have implemented AI in their hiring processes, the study identifies key benefits and challenges associated with these technologies.

One of the main findings of this study is that AI-driven hiring platforms decrease time-to-hire by an average of 40%. These decreases in time-to-hire are due to the automation of labor-intensive tasks, which include resume screening, scheduling interviews, and even preliminary candidate assessments. NLP and machine learning algorithms enable the platform to scan thousands of applications instantly to narrow down the number of applicants that fit the needs of the job. This efficiency allows recruiters to focus on more strategic aspects of talent acquisition, such as relationship-building and organizational fit assessment.

The report also draws attention to how AI is changing candidate satisfaction. AI applications enhance the experience of recruitment through personalization of interactions, real-time updates, and transparency. For example, chatbots and virtual assistants engage candidates by giving them instantaneous responses to queries, application feedback customized according to each applicant's case, and information on the hiring process. These features make the recruitment journey smooth and interesting. This study revealed that as many as 78% of candidates who used AI-enhanced recruitment platforms reported a more positive experience than did 52% who used traditional methods of recruitment.

2.2 GENERATING JOB POSITIONS AND ADS

GenAI revolutionizes how organizations think of putting out job postings and ads. It enables automation for generating job descriptions, ensures proper optimization of the content with search engines, and provides optimal ad personalization toward various platforms and people who view them. An exhaustive account of the implications for these is described next in more detail under important subheadings.

2.2.1 Using AI to Create Job Descriptions

Crafting effective job descriptions is an art and science requiring precision, creativity, and alignment with organizational needs. Job descriptions play a crucial role in attracting the right candidates while setting clear expectations for the role. However, this process is time-consuming, and traditional methods often fail to address issues such as inclusivity and relevance across diverse markets. Generative AI is revolutionizing this domain by automating, refining, and optimizing job descriptions.

2.2.1.1 Efficient Drafting

AI models, such as GPT-4, have the ability to review and process large datasets associated with job roles, industries, and skill requirements. In turn, this allows it to produce detailed, relevant, and precise job descriptions.

- **Keywords Integration**: AI ensures that job descriptions include industry-specific keywords, enhancing clarity and relevance. For example, a data analyst's job description might emphasize keywords such as "data visualization," "Python," or "machine learning."
- **Time-Saving Automation**: AI tools can produce first drafts in minutes, saving the time of the HR teams in manually drafting descriptions.

- **Customizable Outputs**: The HR team inputs details regarding qualifications, responsibilities, and goals of the organization. These are seamlessly infused into the AI draft.

Research indicates that AI-generated job descriptions can be up to 50% faster than traditional hand-drafting processes [8].

2.2.1.2 Inclusive Language

Bias in job descriptions can discourage diverse candidates from applying, thereby limiting the talent pool and perpetuating inequities. GenAI tools address this issue by identifying and eliminating biased or gendered language.

- **Promoting Diversity**: AI-powered platforms such as Textio highlight terms that may unintentionally discourage applications from underrepresented groups. For example, words such as "aggressive negotiator" can be replaced by "strong communicator."
- **Gender-Neutral Language**: AI ensures that neutral language is used, which appeals to all genders. A journal published in the Journal of Business and Psychology reported that job postings with gender-neutral language increased the number of female applicants by 27% [9].
- **Cultural Sensitivity**: In multinational organizations, AI aims to avoid cultural insensitivity, ensuring inclusivity across geographic regions.

Organizations that refine job descriptions to make them inclusive through AI report a jump in applicant diversity of as much as 30%. This is evidenced by platforms such as Skillate [10].

2.2.1.3 Dynamic Updates

The labor market is dynamic, with changing skill demands and industry trends. GenAI allows for the rapid adaptation of job descriptions to keep up with these changes.

- **Tailored for Different Locations**: AI can generate job descriptions that consider local regulations, compensation expectations, and cultural nuances.
- **Role-Specific Variations**: For companies that are hiring for similar positions in different departments or at various levels, AI generates several different versions of a job description. Therefore, an "analyst" role in marketing might highlight analytics tools, whereas one role in finance might be more about quantitative modeling.
- **Responsive to Feedback**: AI systems can integrate feedback from hiring managers or candidates and refine their descriptions over time so that they remain relevant and appealing.

According to Deloitte, research shows that using AI in dynamic updates of job descriptions reduces time-to-market for job postings by 40%. This puts organizations in the best position in tight labor markets.

2.2.2 Search Engine (SEO)-Optimized Job Postings

Competition among jobs has increased, and the efficiency with which job postings reach the right candidates is important for appropriate recruitment. SEO increases the search engine and job board exposure of job postings. Advanced generations of AI enhance this entire process by automating or optimizing SEO techniques to make job postings more effective in their impact.

- **Keywords Optimization**: The use of keywords is one of the most basic practices in SEO. AI tools are best suited for analyzing big data and identifying the most relevant and high-performing keywords on the basis of job titles, industry standards, and specific skills.
- **Targeted Keyword Research**: RankAI and SEMrush are AI-driven tools that analyze search trends and identify keywords that candidates often use when searching for similar roles. For example, for a "software developer" role, keywords such as "full-stack developer," "JavaScript," or "remote software engineer jobs" may be prioritized.
- **Semantic Relevance**: AI goes beyond exact matches, identifying semantically related terms that enhance searchability. For example, "data scientist" might be accompanied by terms such as "machine learning specialist" or "big data analyst."
- **Dynamic Updates**: AI continuously monitors search trends and updates the job posting with trending keywords to keep it relevant and visible throughout.

Studies indicate that if these job postings contain AI-suggested keywords, the likelihood of increasing their appearance on a job board can increase by up to 50% with higher rates of application [8].

2.2.2.1 Content Structuring

Proper structuring of content not only improves SEO rankings but also enhances the readability and engagement of job postings. GenAI ensures that job descriptions are formatted and organized to meet SEO and user experience standards.

- **Clear Headings and Subheadings**: AI tools help structure job descriptions with concise, keyword-rich headings, making them easier to navigate. For example:
    - *Job Title: Software developers*
    - *Responsibilities: Developing scalable web applications*
    - *Requirements: Proficiency in JavaScript, Python, and React.*
- **Bullet Points and Lists**: AI prefers to make use of bullet points when listing duties, qualifications, and benefits, as they increase readability and help search engines index content better.
- **Readable Length**: AI posts are not too wordy and break information into digestible sections that appeal to readers and are within the bounds of search engine recommendations.

Organizations that use AI to structure job postings report better user engagement. The time spent on job postings increased by 30% because of improved readability.

2.2.2.2 Meta Tags and Descriptions

Meta tags and descriptions are critical to SEO, as they create a snapshot of the job posting to users as well as to search engines. GenAI simplifies effective meta-content creation to increase the CTR.

- **Optimized Meta Descriptions**: AI generates short summaries to present job postings with strong interest, often involving main keywords and calls-to-action such as "Apply now for this great software engineering opportunity with the world's leading technology firm!"
- **Schema Markup**: Advanced AI tools integrate schema markup, which provides structured data to search engines, hence improving the way job postings are displayed on platforms such as Google for Jobs.
- **Title Tag Optimization**: AI ensures that job titles are SEO-friendly, concise, and include keywords that candidates are likely to search for, such as "Remote Senior Software Developer – Python/Java."

According to Moz's report, meta descriptions and tags can be optimized more effectively to increase click rates by up to 30%, thus driving more traffic to a job posting. Figure 2.1 shows the effectiveness of various SEO techniques, such as keyword optimization, the structuring of content, and the use of meta tags, in improving the visibility of a job posting.

2.2.3 Customized Job Ads for Different Platforms

With multiplatform recruitment, the success of job advertisements depends on how well they align with the unique characteristics of the platform and audience preferences. Generative AI empowers organizations to create job advertisements tailored to

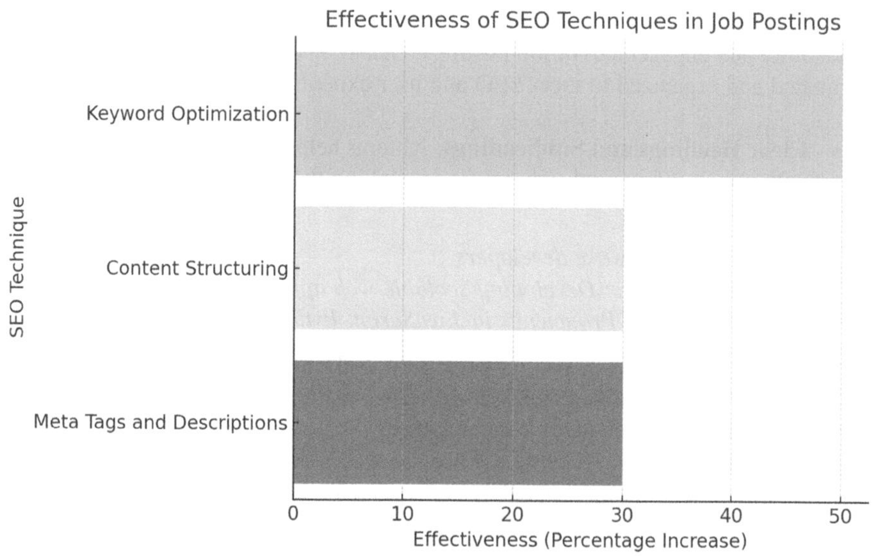

FIGURE 2.1 Effectiveness of SEO techniques in job postings.

maximize visibility and engagement on platforms such as LinkedIn, Glassdoor, and social media channels such as Instagram and Facebook.

2.2.3.1 Key Features of Customization

1. **Platform-Specific Formatting**: Every platform has different rules and audience expectations. GenAI creates advertisements that meet these requirements automatically.
   - *LinkedIn*: Text-intensive with a professional tone and career development focus.
   - *Instagram*: Visual-heavy with concise captions and an informal tone.
   - *Twitter*: Brief, engaging text within character limits, often incorporating trending hashtags.
2. **Audience Segmentation**: GenAI uses data analytics to segment audiences on the basis of demographic factors such as the following:
   - Location (local job ads vs. global roles).
   - Job level (entry-level, mid-level, or executive).
   - Industry focus (tech, healthcare, marketing, etc.).
3. **Dynamic Updates**: AI-powered systems monitor engagement metrics, including clicks, impressions, and shares, and adjust ads in real time to optimize performance. For instance:
   - The tone is adjusted to be more formal if professional engagement is low.
   - The visuals are updated with more dynamic elements, such as videos or infographics, on the basis of audience preferences (Table 2.1).

2.2.4 Personalizing Job Advertisements

The personalization of job advertisements is key to attracting top talent in a competitive job market. GenAI uses data to create job advertisements that resonate with specific audiences.

- **Tailored Messaging**: AI tools analyze data on candidate preferences, such as desired benefits or company culture, to craft personalized messages.
- **Adaptive Content**: AI systems vary language and tone according to the targeted demographic, for example, formal language for senior positions and casual language for entry-level positions.
- **Localized Ads**: For multinational organizations, AI can create location-specific ads that incorporate cultural nuances, local benefits, and regional language.

According to a report by Deloitte, personalized job ads increase candidate engagement by 35% and are more likely to attract applications from qualified candidates.

2.2.5 Job Ad Performance Analytics

Creating effective job advertisements is only one half of the equation; measuring their performance is just as important. GenAI tools provide insights into ad performance that help optimize the recruitment strategies of HR teams.

TABLE 2.1
Examples of Customized Job Ads Across Platforms

Platform	Ad Format	Tone	Target Audience	Unique Features	Example
LinkedIn	Text-heavy, professional graphics	Formal, career-focused	Professionals, industry experts	Detailed descriptions, career growth opportunities	"Join our growing team of data analysts and thrive in a dynamic workspace."
Instagram	Visually engaging posts/ stories	Conversational, informal	Younger talent, creatives	High-quality visuals, short captions	"Dream job alert! 🌟 Join us for exciting projects and cool perks."
Indeed	Structured job postings with bullet points	Neutral, clear	Broad audience, job seekers	Straightforward, keyword-rich content	"Exciting opportunity: Project Manager role at XYZ Co. Apply now!"
Twitter	Snappy tweets with hashtags	Trendy, engaging	Tech-savvy, fast-paced audience	Brevity, hashtags, and trending topics	"Looking for a change? 🚀 Check out our openings in tech: #TechJobs #Careers"
Facebook	Mixed text and visuals	Friendly, community-driven	Local job seekers	Targeted ads, community-oriented messaging	"We're hiring locally! Join our team and make an impact in your community."
Glassdoor	Transparent reviews + job postings	Honest, straightforward	Professionals researching companies	Detailed company culture insights	"Learn what makes XYZ Co. a top workplace. Apply today!"

TABLE 2.2
Visualizing Job Ad Performance Analytics

Feature	Description	Example Tools	Benefits
Engagement metrics	Tracks impressions, clicks, and application rates.	Google Ads AI, LinkedIn Campaign Manager	Identifies underperforming ads.
A/B testing	Tests variants to find the best-performing version.	LinkedIn Campaign Manager	Optimizes messaging for higher engagement.
Real-time feedback	Provides actionable insights into performance trends.	Google Ads AI	Enables on-the-fly adjustments for better results.

- **Engagement Metrics**: AI follows metrics such as impressions, clicks, and application rates to determine how effective a job ad is.
- **A/B Testing**: AI tools can help with A/B testing of variants of job advertisements, thus helping identify which one drives the most engagement or applications.
- **Real-Time Feedback**: AI-based analytics provides real-time insights so that the HR team can change ads to optimize them better.

For example, Google Ads AI and the LinkedIn Campaign Manager use AI analytics to determine the most effective keywords and optimize budget distribution, increasing the Return on Investment ROI by up to 50% (Table 2.2).

This comprehensive approach toward job ad performance analytics ensures that HR teams create engaging ads and, simultaneously, continually refine their strategies to attract the best talent effectively.

2.3 AI-POWERED RESUME SCREENING AND FILTERING

The recruitment process can be significantly streamlined via AI-powered tools for resume screening and filtering. This approach not only saves time but also enhances the accuracy and fairness of candidate selection. Subsequently, we explore the key subsections that detail the functionalities and benefits of AI in this domain.

2.3.1 Automating Resume Parsing and Data Extraction

AI-powered tools for resume screening and filtering can help streamline the recruitment process to a great extent. This approach not only saves time but also increases the accuracy and fairness of candidate selection [11]. We discuss the major subheadings later, detailing the functionalities and benefits of AI in this domain.

These technologies form the basis for this capability, including NLP and Optical Character Recognition (OCR), which allow the AI system to understand human language so that it can extract contextually relevant information pertaining to job roles or specific skill sets. OCR helps in converting resumes from image-based sources, making even noneditable formats readable and usable in AI systems. Thus, these technologies form a more robust framework for parsing all kinds of resume formats.

There are numerous advantages to resume parsing automation. This approach saves considerable time and resources for HR teams in terms of the effort involved in data entry. Additionally, AI is known to process large volumes of resumes with unmatched efficiency and will never miss any critical information in the process. This not only speeds up the screening process but also ensures that the data are accurate and ready for subsequent analysis and matching steps.

2.3.2 Enhancing Screening Accuracy with AI

AI-powered tools ensure that resume screening has a high level of precision by using complex algorithms and matching candidates with job requirements. These tools compare the information extracted with the job descriptions to determine which candidate best suits the role. These AI systems score resumes in terms of keywords, level of experience, and educational qualifications of the person. AI goes beyond basic matching to keywords, uses the contextual relevance of a candidate's skills and experiences, and performs semantic analysis. Then, machine learning algorithms are applied for accuracy, which builds with time because of such feedback loops.

This technological precision reduces the chances of false positives and false negatives in candidate selection. Highly qualified candidates, who may have otherwise gone unnoticed during manual screening, are identified, thereby improving the quality of the applicant pool. With these developments, organizations can make more informed and confident hiring decisions.

2.3.3 Mitigating Bias in the Resume Filtering Process

AI can also eliminate one of the most significant and persistent problems in traditional hiring processes: bias [12]. AI systems focus more on objective criteria such as skills and experience, thus eliminating demographic factors such as name, gender, or ethnicity that might influence the hiring process. In fact, some AI-based tools anonymize resumes fully, removing all identifying information to ensure a fair evaluation process. These practices are rooted within fairness-aware machine learning and other ethical AI frameworks designed for the detection of bias, potentially in algorithms.

This increases diversity and inclusion by showing equal opportunities to all candidates. It also reduces the number of cases of violations related to antidiscrimination laws and builds trust in the hiring process. With bias-mitigation techniques in their AI systems, organizations commit to fair and equitable hiring practices.

2.3.4 Improving Efficiency and Accuracy in Hiring

AI tools greatly increase the efficiency of hiring by automating tasks that are time-consuming and optimizing workflows. For example, they can process thousands of

TABLE 2.3
Summary Table

Subsection	Key Functionality	Technologies Involved	Advantages
Automating resume parsing	Extracts structured data from resumes	NLP [13], OCR	Saves time and reduces manual effort.
Enhancing screening accuracy	Matches resumes with job requirements	Machine learning, semantic analysis	Improves precision in candidate selection.
Mitigating bias	Removes identifying details to reduce bias	Fairness-aware machine learning, ethical AI	Promotes diversity and inclusion.
Improving efficiency and accuracy	Speeds up shortlisting and enhances accuracy	Predictive analytics, ATS integration	Improves hiring quality and efficiency.

resumes in just minutes, allowing HR teams to concentrate their efforts on strategic decision-making and candidate engagement. Predictive analytics further enhance hiring outcomes by identifying the most likely candidates to succeed on the basis of historical data and performance trends.

Moreover, they integrate with Applicant Tracking System ATSs, thus streamlining processes for recruiters. AI real-time insights allow for adjustments in recruitment strategies immediately to improve the quality of hires while reducing time-to-hire. With these automated and optimized processes, AI allows organizations to achieve better hiring outcomes with fewer resources (Table 2.3).

By leveraging these AI-powered capabilities, organizations can revolutionize their hiring processes, ensuring fairness, efficiency, and quality in candidate selection.

2.4 ENHANCING JOB SEEKER EXPERIENCE WITH AI TECHNOLOGY

AI technology has transformed the recruitment landscape and improved the experience of job seekers. Organizations are now better positioned to connect with candidates through personalized recommendations, AI-powered support systems, interactive assessments, and advanced feedback collection mechanisms. We explain these subsections in detail subsequently.

2.4.1 Personalized Job Recommendations

The most impactful application of AI in recruitment is the ability to provide personalized job recommendations. AI platforms use machine learning algorithms and NLP to analyze a candidate's resume, job application history, and browsing behavior on job portals. This allows for the creation of a tailored list of opportunities that match the candidate's skills, preferences, and career aspirations.

For example, LinkedIn and Glassdoor use collaborative filtering and content-based filtering to determine job roles. Research papers such as [14] describe how hybrid approaches, which combine collaborative filtering with NLP, improve the accuracy of job matching. These systems not only improve the user experience but also help employers connect with the most motivated candidates by making job hunting more efficient and relevant.

2.4.2 AI-Powered Support: Virtual Assistants and Chatbots

AI-powered virtual assistants and chatbots have become significant modern recruitment tools that change the way organizations engage with job seekers. Intelligent systems use NLP to understand and answer candidate queries in a manner that is similar to that of a human being so that applicants receive accurate and timely information. Automating routine interactions enhances the efficiency of communication and reduces the workload of HR teams, which then enables them to focus on more strategic tasks. Another key advantage of AI chatbots is that they can work around the clock and provide 24/7 support to job seekers, regardless of time zones or geographical locations. This capability is exemplified by Olivia and HireVue, which allow seamless support throughout the recruitment journey. These chatbots guide candidates through the application process, help them navigate job portals, and even schedule interviews so that applicants are kept engaged and informed.

In addition to answering FAQs, AI-powered virtual assistants can personalize interactions by analyzing a candidate's profile and tailoring responses to their specific needs. For example, a chatbot may recommend suitable job openings, explain role requirements, or provide tips for successful applications on the basis of a candidate's experience and skills. Real-time updates on application statuses further improve transparency, fostering trust and satisfaction among job seekers. Accessibility has also improved through the integration of conversational AI in recruitment. Since conversational AI supports various languages and features intuitive interfaces that are easy to use, chatbots allow a more diverse population of users to participate in employment platforms. In addition, advancements in sentiment analysis empower these systems to understand candidate tone or mood and create empathetic responses on the basis of context.

2.4.3 AI-Based Interactive Assessments

AI-based interactive assessments are changing the dynamics of old-school methods of evaluation and creating new interactive experiences for candidates. They differ from traditional static tests, as they involve several types of interviews. Assessments with advanced AI algorithms evaluate candidate attributes such as problem-solving skills, personalities, communication skills, and emotional quotients. The tools incorporate elements of gamification, simulations, and video interviews, making the entire assessment process more enjoyable for candidates while providing richer data for recruiters.

Examples of the power of AI in this domain include Pymetrics and HireVue Insights [15]. Pymetrics uses neuroscience-based games to evaluate cognitive and emotional traits, matching candidates to roles where they are most likely to succeed. Similarly, HireVue Insights uses video interviews combined with AI analysis to assess verbal and nonverbal cues, such as tone of voice, word choice, and facial expressions. These insights allow organizations to go beyond resumes, achieving a deeper understanding of an applicant's potential.

Gamification plays a crucial role in increasing engagement and decreasing the stress levels of assessment takers. Challenges are presented in a game-like format, and candidates have an opportunity to present themselves in a relaxed, interactive manner. The simulations, however, provide a realistic view, and the candidate is evaluated on the basis of their decision-making and adaptability, offering a glimpse into how the candidate might perform in actual situations. By embracing AI-based interactive assessments, organizations can make the hiring process more inclusive and engaging for top talent, align it with data-driven business objectives, and ensure the effective evaluation of candidates through fairer and more effective recruitment practices.

2.4.4 Collecting and Analyzing Candidate Feedback

AI also plays a very important role in collecting and analyzing candidate feedback so that organizations can refine their recruitment strategies. Sentiment analysis algorithms process the feedback data collected through surveys or chatbots, identifying key areas for improvement in the hiring process. This ensures that organizations stay aligned with candidates' expectations, fostering trust and long-term engagement.

For example, the study by [16] examined how AI could be used in recognizing trends and patterns of candidate satisfaction. More sophisticated applications of AI, such as those utilized in Qualtrics and SurveyMonkey, automatically analyze feedback for HR teams to provide them with actionable insights that are easier to integrate into organizational changes. Implementing AI technology in job searching not only improves candidate experiences but also helps improve employer branding and recruiting. All this is possible by integrating the organization's processes with personalized job recommendations, AI-powered support systems, interactive assessments, and feedback analysis to create a more engaging and effective hiring journey. With advancements built on the latest research, it is clear that the use of AI in recruitment is transformative.

REFERENCES

1. Gupta, C. P., & Kumar, V. V. R. (2024). Artificial intelligence application in human resource management: The way forward. *2024 ASU International Conference in Emerging Technologies for Sustainability and Intelligent Systems (ICETSIS)*, Manama, Bahrain, pp. 1726–1730. https://doi.org/10.1109/ICETSIS61505.2024.10459605
2. Babuji, S., Mathew, T., Pooja, T., Karibeeran, S., & Saravanan, V. (2025). AI-driven human resource management: Enhancing talent acquisition, employee relations and workforce development. *International Journal of Research in Management*, 7, 320–327. https://doi.org/10.33545/26648792.2025.v7.i1d.294
3. Upadhyay, A. K., & Khandelwal, K. (2018). Applying artificial intelligence: Implications for recruitment. *Strategic HR Review*, 17(5), 255–258. https://doi.org/10.1108/SHR-07-2018-0051

4. Gartner. (2023). https://www.gartner.com/en/newsroom/press-releases/20222-08-29-gartner-hr-finds-59-percent-of-candidates-would-still-accept-job-offer
5. Smith, A., et al. (2020). Data analytics in HR management. *HR Science Review.*
6. Deloitte. (2020). Workforce strategies for post COVID-19 recovery. https://www.deloitte.com/global/en/issues/resilience/covid-19-workforce-strategies-for-post-covid-recovery.html
7. Kiran, L., et al. (2022). Impact of AI on recruitment processes. *Journal of Business AI Applications.*
8. Tambe, P., Cappelli, P., & Yakubovich, V. (2019). Artificial intelligence in human resources management: Challenges and a path forward. *California Management Review*, 61(4), 15–42. https://doi.org/10.1177/0008125619867910
9. Gaucher, D., Friesen, J., & Kay, A. C. (2011). Evidence that gendered wording in job advertisements exists and sustains gender inequality. *Journal of Personality and Social Psychology*, 101(1), 109–128. https://doi.org/10.1037/a0022530
10. https://www.skillate.com/features/diversity-and-inclusion/
11. Rajesh, B., & Mrinal, S. (2024). Resume screening app using AI. *International Journal of Latest Technology in Engineering Management & Applied Science*, 13(6), 13–16. https://doi.org/10.51583/IJLTEMAS.2024.130602.
12. Sipior, J. C., Ward, B. T., Rusinko, C. A., & Lombardi, D. R. (2023). Bias in using AI for recruiting: Legal considerations. *Information Systems Management*, 41(4), 399–412. https://doi.org/10.1080/10580530.2023.2294453
13. Akram, N., Majeed, A., Khan, S., Salam, Z. A. A., Sohail, A., & Shahbaz, S. (2023). Automation of resume classification using machine learning algorithm. In *2023 IEEE 21st Student Conference on Research and Development (SCOReD)*, Kuala Lumpur, Malaysia, December 2023 (pp. 403–407). https://doi.org/10.1109/SCOReD60679.2023.10563408
14. Mulay, A., Sutar, S., Patel, J., Chhabria, A., & Mumbaikar, S. (2022). Job recommendation system using hybrid filtering. *ITM Web of Conferences*, 44, 02002. https://doi.org/10.1051/itmconf/20224402002
15. Khosravy, M., Gupta, N., Pasquali, A., Dey, N., Crespo, R. G., & Witkowski, O. (2023). Human-collaborative artificial intelligence along with social values in industry 5.0: A survey of the state-of-the-art. *IEEE Transactions on Cognitive and Developmental Systems*, 16(1), 165–176.
16. Mishra, A., Singh, S., & Jisha, R. C. (2024). AI-powered model for intelligent resume recommendation and feedback. In *2024 15th International Conference on Computing Communication and Networking Technologies (ICCCNT)*, Kamand, India, June 2024 (pp. 1–6). https://doi.org/10.1109/ICCCNT61001.2024.10726016

3 Efficient Onboarding and Training to Facilitate Employee Success

This chapter offers a critical review of the design and implementation of onboarding and recurrent training programs, which act as central instruments for achieving immediate employee incorporation and long-term workforce ability within organizations. Onboarding has traditionally been framed as a transitory process oriented toward accelerating role acquisition and socialization; however, contemporary academic literature focuses on its strategic value for enhancing retention, organizational commitment, and overall employee well-being. In the same vein, recurrent training and development have moved on from being considered secondary human resource (HR) procedures and have instead assumed critical paradigms for sustaining organizational flexibility within contexts defined by advances in technology, shifting labor markets, and evolving skill demands.

The chapter places its analysis in this deeper context, tracing the ways in which newly arriving digital technologies—primarily automation and artificial intelligence (AI)—are remaking the workforce learning ends and means. In particular, it examines the pros and cons of automated onboarding programs that promise efficiency, consistency, and large-scale personalization but also pose questions about inclusivity, worker autonomy, and communication in the context of organizational culture. The discussion then proceeds to AI-based training and development and examines the role of adaptive learning systems, algorithmic personalization, and predictive analytics in defining career paths and distributing organizational knowledge. These interventions come under critical review both in terms of their functional performance and through an investigation of ethical, epistemological, and representational questions around their use.

A considerable example is given for the development of measurement frameworks that could be used to measure the immediate and long-term effects of onboarding and training interventions. Traditional metrics such as completion rates or time-to-productivity undergo critical scrutiny alongside more advanced metrics that gauge transfer of learning, retention of skills, and building organizational capabilities. It is argued that without rigorous evaluative structures in place, organizations may fall into a pattern of valuing speed over the real value of workforce development and, hence, undermine its potential for strategic application.

Grounding the theoretical discussions in practice, the chapter then explores the implementation of automated and AI-supported interventions within organizations by means of a case study. The case study is not presented as a best practice; rather, it acts as an empirical filter through which the tensions, trade-offs, and contingencies of implementation are brought into view.

DOI: 10.1201/9781003674887-3

The chapter ultimately aims to add to the academic dialogue at the crossroads of human resource management (HRM), organizational learning, and AI. The chapter sets out as particularly relevant to HR leaders and learning and development practitioners in search of evidence-informed practices and the implications for researchers concerned with the ethical, social, and organizational responsibilities of training a workforce in AI. This chapter adopts a critical and pragmatic stance; it focuses on issues of effectiveness and scalability while being mindful of the broader theoretical and normative implications of workforce development within algorithmic management.

3.1 AUTOMATED ONBOARDING PROGRAMS

Onboarding is a pivotal stage in the employment life cycle because new employees' first impressions of organizational culture, norms, expectations, and career direction form at this stage. Traditionally, onboarding has been accomplished face-to-face, through paper, and less formally, through mentoring structures. However, with increasing pressure on organizations for scalability, efficiency, and consistency with dispersed and diverse workforces, automated onboarding is a viable alternative.

Automated onboarding uses technology and workflow platforms to help automate onboarding processes, provide digital learning modules in support of a streamlined learning program, and allow for a personalized experience on the basis of the needs of the new hire with the help of data. By automating some of the mundane activities, such as document submission, compliance training, and scheduling, the HR team can facilitate a smooth onboarding process while ensuring that new employees receive resources and information in a timely manner. More sophisticated systems leverage adaptive learning paths, chatbots, and AI-based recommendation systems to provide an ongoing resource of engagement by providing cues for the employee beyond the first day and facilitating an onboarding process that extends over time into a structured professional development path.

Positioned theoretically, automated onboarding represents a transition from socialization activities grounded in human interactions to technology-assisted entry into an organization. The shift toward automation brings several potential advantages, including efficiency, cost-effectiveness, and standardization across locations, but raises key issues, including relational depth, equity, and the sharing of tacit knowledge. Scholars have cautioned that using automation too much may lead the onboarding process to be a compliance-driven task and overlook the affective, cultural, and identity-based aspects of socialization, which are often necessary for long-term retention and engagement.

For this subsection, we analyze the design and use of automated onboarding programs, as they relate to efficiency, advantages, and drawbacks in relation to employee experience, equity, and organizational culture. We analyze automated onboarding by providing both conceptual framing for understanding onboarding automation and practical perspectives on how organizations can achieve the efficiency of technology while also applying the human aspects of managing employee onboarding.

3.1.1 Designing Customized Onboarding Programs with AI Tools

The contemporary design of onboarding programs has shifted from a transactional compliance and administrative efficiency orientation toward a strategic and customized approach that is consonant with integration, learning, and long-term retention [1, 2]. Contemporary developments in AI, process automation, and digital HR technologies enable the creation of onboarding experiences that can be dynamic, data-driven, and highly integrated with comprehensive talent management systems [3, 4]. Compared with the previously static checklist- and session-based orientation of onboarding, modern designs emphasize customization, role-based flows, and enterprise-wide stakeholder alignment.

3.1.1.1 Preboarding Automation

Preboarding signifies a pivotal yet frequently disregarded phase of the onboarding process. Automating aspects of the administrative onboarding process can facilitate faster integration into the organization with respect to completing new employee paperwork, acknowledging employee policies, and distributing materials and tools. Digital workflows help reduce errors, reduce administrative lag, and ensure compliance on behalf of employees prior to their first day of work. Research indicates that timely, formalized connections contribute to developing psychological safety as well as the perception that the organization is prepared for the new employee, both of which have been shown to predict newcomer adjustment outcomes [5, 6].

3.1.1.2 Role-based Learning Pathways

AI-enabled systems allow for the creation of role-based learning pathways by ordering the microlearning modules in relation to an employee's role, level of seniority, and past experience. In addition, the learning pathways can be adjusted dynamically on the basis of performance, engagement, and knowledge retention metrics via machine-learning algorithms [7]. This is consistent with skill-based workforce strategies that focus on developing employees not only in accordance with job titles but also in relation to the competencies and capabilities that align with the development of their careers and the organization's initiatives and goals [8].

3.1.1.3 Personalized Schedules and Adaptive Guidance

The personalization afforded by AI exceeds learning content and includes scheduling and resource allocation. Automated calendar integration allows organizations to create personal schedules leveraging compliance training, role-specific modules, mentoring sessions, Outlook calendars, and introductions to team members. Virtual assistants with natural language generation (NLG) capabilities can generate customized welcome messages, personalized to-do lists, and personalized reminders. Research has shown that this level of personalization increases engagement and decreases time-to-productivity because it shifts organizational processes to be responsive to the needs and expectations of employees.

3.1.1.4 Stakeholder Orchestration

Effective onboarding involves more than just HR, as line managers, IT, facilities, and peer mentors must work together. AI-enabled workflows can help orchestrate between stakeholders, automatically triggering tasks and transferring data in HR information systems (HRISs), learning management systems (LMSs), IT tickets, and payroll applications. RPA (robotic process automation) and workflow engines ensure that logistical dependencies (setting up accounts, access to systems, setting up desks, etc.) occur in parallel rather than in sequence, eliminating unnecessary delays or bottlenecks.

3.1.1.5 AI Tools and Capabilities

AI consists of a set of technologies that are increasingly central to the development and implementation of customized onboarding programs. Rather than operating as discrete technical elements, they reside within a broader-based sociotechnical system that changes the means by which organizations monitor, integrate, and support newly recruited staff [4]. The following categories of AI tools are particularly relevant for onboarding purposes:

- **NLG**: NLG tools can generate text-based communications for individual new hires, such as welcome messages, role introductions, and adaptive to-do lists. By relying on organizational data (e.g., job role, prior experience, department, etc.), NLG can customize the content for each new employee, thereby creating a sense of individualized interaction in a scalable manner. NLG is not only functional but also symbolic: the use of personalized text communicates a sense of concern and responsiveness from the organization and has been associated with stronger affective commitment and outcomes of early socialization in research [5]. However, reliance on generated text creates challenges regarding authenticity and relational depth, particularly within cultures of onboarding where interpersonal contact is valued.
- **Recommendation Engines**: Recommendation engines use collaborative filtering models and machine-learning algorithms from e-commerce and digital media to recommend resources related to new hires' roles (e.g., learning modules, policies, mentor pairings, etc.) [7, 9]. In onboarding, the recommendation engine function works by building adaptive, role-focused learning pathways in response to organizational expectations and the profile of the new employee. The assumed strength of this algorithm is that it allows for personalization at scale, whereby each new employee receives recommendations reflective of their role and professional development journey. However, scholars of algorithmic management caution that such systems may inadvertently embed organizational biases or channel employees into rigid pathways that constrain agency.
- **Process Automation (RPA and Workflow Engines)**: Both RPA and workflow orchestration systems enable seamless connectivity between disparate organizational systems, including HRISs, LMSs, IT ticketing, and payroll applications. These technologies automate repetitive and rule-based tasks such as account provisioning, payroll enrollment, or compliance tracking,

thus reducing administrative error and accelerating access to key systems. From an efficiency perspective, RPA lowers transaction costs and frees HR staff from administrative tasks to focus on the strategic, relational, and developmental aspects of onboarding. From a sociotechnical perspective, however, it also reflects a change in the division of labor between humans and machines, thus raising important considerations about the deskilling of work, employee autonomy, and the potential for the overstandardization of onboarding practices.

The comparative analysis presented in Table 3.1 suggests that, while AI tools each represent a different functional contribution to onboarding, ranging from communicative personalization (NLG) to adaptive guidance (recommendation engines) and workflow efficiency (RPA), the true value of these tools is in their collective role in a sociotechnical system that produces onboarding processes that are more scalable and efficient, as well as more personalized and adaptive in nature. Moreover, the aforementioned risks across research categories highlight a common set of challenges related to authenticity, equity, and transparency for algorithmically mediated HR practices. The tension between efficiency gains and relational/ethical considerations therefore appears to be a definitive quality of AI-enabled onboarding. From an academic perspective, these tools ought not to be viewed simply as technical capabilities but as interventions that alter the logic of organizational entry and impact how newcomers experience work, how organizations communicate culture, and how power plays out between humans and intelligent systems.

3.1.1.6 Implementation Checklist

To actualize these programs, organizations should develop an organized plan for design and execution as follows:

1. Map the comprehensive experience of new hires (preboarding → day 1 → 30/60/90 milestones).
2. Identify opportunities for automation and personalization while being cognizant of organizational needs and employee expectations.
3. Interoperable tools that integrate HRISs, LMSs, and virtual agents are acquired [3, 4].
4. A skills-first pathway is created for each role with a focus on competencies and less focus on static job descriptions [8].
5. Pilots with a small cohort, qualitative and quantitative feedback, and iterative redesign based on pilot outcomes are included.

While the potential benefits of AI-enabled onboarding processes are significant, they create crucial challenges to consider before they are introduced. The algorithms tasked with personalizing the onboarding experience risk replicating existing biases if the training dataset is not representative. Actions aimed at overautomating parts of the onboarding experience may limit relational socialization opportunities for new hires and tacit job knowledge, which may be imperative for fostering commitment to the organization. In addition, the issues of transparency, explainability, and employee trust are consequential for the acceptance of AI-mediated decision-making

TABLE 3.1
AI Tools and Capabilities in Onboarding Programs

AI Tool	Primary Function	Organizational Benefits	Potential Risks/Limitations	Key References
NLG	Produces individualized communications (e.g., welcome messages, to-do lists, role introductions).	- Creates personalized experiences at scale. - Enhances newcomer engagement and perceived organizational support. - Reduces time burden on HR staff.	- Risk of perceived inauthenticity in automated messages. - Limited relational depth compared to human interaction. - Potential cultural mismatch in high-touch organizational settings.	[5]
Recommendation engines	Suggest role-relevant resources (e.g., learning modules, mentors, documents).	- Supports adaptive, role-based learning pathways. - Enables mass personalization of training and development. - Accelerates skill acquisition and role integration.	- May embed or reproduce existing biases. - Potential to constrain employee agency by narrowing recommended choices. - Algorithmic opacity may reduce trust.	[7, 9]
Process automation (RPA/workflow engines)	Automates workflows across HRIS, LMS, IT, payroll, and compliance systems.	- Streamlines administrative processes. - Reduces errors and delays in system access. - Frees HR professionals for higher-value strategic tasks.	- Overstandardization of onboarding experiences. - Risk of deskilling HR staff by automating routine knowledge. - Technical failures may create bottlenecks across systems.	[10]

processes. Finally, even with a high degree of efficiency and automation in organizational scenarios, organizations should consider ethics and the role that onboarding plays in the humanization of employee transitions to the organization.

3.1.2 Virtual Onboarding Assistants and Tools

Integrating virtual assistants and technology into onboarding programs provides an innovative solution for onboarding individuals into the workforce, taking advantage of AI for urgent support, personalized support, and ongoing interactions. Virtual onboarding assistants, typically powered by chatbots, natural language processing (NLP), and machine learning, act as virtual brokers to assist new employees through the onboarding sequence, answer questions, and help accomplish necessary tasks.

Virtual onboarding assistants have several primary functions that promote efficiency and employee experience:

- **Information Delivery and FAQs**: AI chatbots can answer frequently asked questions related to company and employee policy, employee benefits, IT permissions, and compliance while limiting human intervention.
- **Workflow Guidance and Task Orchestration**: Virtual assistants are able to track and remind employees of onboarding tasks and deadlines, tasks completed, and training required and can integrate with HRISs, LMSs, and calendaring systems easily.
- **Personalized Development and Learning**: Virtual assistants offer personalized onboarding experiences on the basis of the role and previous experience of the employee through recommendations for competence-based learning, mentoring experiences, and articles to read.
- **Feedback and Engagement Monitoring**: Virtual assistants can accept organized feedback from newcomers, track engagement metrics, and flag issues for follow-up in real time, providing HR with actionable insights (Table 3.2).

TABLE 3.2
Functions and Benefits of Virtual Onboarding Assistants

Function	Description	Organizational Benefits
Information delivery and FAQs	Provides instant answers to policy, benefits, and IT questions.	Reduces HR workload; improves employee confidence and clarity.
Task guidance and workflow	Tracks onboarding milestones, sends reminders, coordinates tasks across HRIS and LMS.	Ensures timely completion of onboarding; reduces bottlenecks; improves process consistency.
Personalized learning and development	Suggests role-specific modules, mentors, and reading resources using recommendation engines.	Enhances learning relevance; accelerates skill acquisition; increases engagement.
Feedback and engagement monitoring	Collects feedback, tracks engagement, flags early retention risks.	Enables data-driven adjustments; supports early intervention strategies.

3.1.3 Measuring the Effectiveness of Virtual Onboarding Programs

The utilization of virtual assistants and AI-driven tools must include strong measurement systems to assess their effectiveness. While necessary, traditional measures of productivity, such as completion rates or time-to-productivity rates, are limited in their ability to capture the broad effects of automated onboarding and employee experience, as well as long-term performance. The relevant measurement dimensions to be included address the following areas:

- **Engagement Measures**: Interactions with virtual assistants, completion of tasks recommended by the virtual assistant, and engagement in learning modules.
- **Knowledge Acquisition and Retention**: Assessment scores, demonstration of skills, alignment with role competencies.
- **Behavioral and Performance Outcomes**: Performance ratings assigned early in employment, time-to-full-productivity rates, and compliance requirement metrics.
- **Employee Experience and Satisfaction**: Levels of onboarding satisfaction, perceptions of support, and organizational commitment.
- **Retention and Attrition Metrics**: Voluntary turnover rates within 6–12 months of employment (Table 3.3).

Although there are many advantages to virtual onboarding assistance, that is, scalability, personalized experiences, and data collection (tracking in real time), these advantages also need to be considered alongside their potential limitations.

TABLE 3.3
Key Metrics for Evaluating Virtual Onboarding Effectiveness

Measurement Dimension	Indicator Examples	Purpose/Insight
Engagement	Number of chatbot interactions; completion of task reminders; use of recommended learning resources	Indicates adoption and utilization of virtual tools; reflects engagement levels
Knowledge acquisition	Scores on role-specific assessments; microlearning completion rates; observed skill demonstration	Evaluates learning transfer and preparedness for role responsibilities
Behavioral and performance outcomes	Time-to-productivity; early performance reviews; compliance completion	Measures alignment of onboarding with organizational performance objectives
Employee experience	Onboarding satisfaction surveys; perceived support; feedback collected via AI assistants	Assesses subjective experience and psychological adjustment
Retention and attrition	Turnover rates within first 6–12 months	Provides long-term indication of onboarding success and integration

One potential drawback is that organizations rely too heavily on AI-enabled communication and minimize relational communication, which stifles socialization or cultural immersion. Algorithm recommendation systems can embed biases into support systems and recommend courses of action, paths of learning, or mentors more than others do [11]. Monitoring employees continuously leads to potential erosion of the ethical agreement regarding privacy, the security of data, and fair and transparent decision-making by AI.

Effective onboarding programs need to reflect an equilibrium between technology efficiency and the human factor, amalgamating automated responses with opportunities for interpersonal engagement, mentorship, and the value of organizational learning.

The metrics and frameworks used to evaluate the success of different types of virtual onboarding programs readily translate to the field of AI-enabled workplace training and development. Just as we assess the success of onboarding in terms of levels of engagement, levels of knowledge acquisition, behavioral outcomes, and employee experience, AI-enabled workplace learning and training initiatives are evaluated in the exact same way in terms of the impact on learning, skills developed, and the organization's overall ability to build learning and development into its business practice.

3.2 AI-DRIVEN TRAINING AND DEVELOPMENT

Training and development have long served to construct organizational capacity, maintain competitiveness, and promote employee development. However, traditional methods focused on standardized curricula, episodic delivery, and limited flexibility have struggled to reskill people in the changing skill demand environment. The emergence of AI has opened new hopes for continuous, adaptive, and individual learning environments. With machine learning, natural language processing, and predictive analytics, an AI system can tailor content to individual learning styles, project skill gaps beginning to emerge, and link development pathways with high-level workforce planning.

This section reviews the important characteristics, affordances, and challenges presented by AI-based training and development methodologies and considers how intelligent systems can take the expected efficiency criteria and move beyond that logic to reconfigure workplace learning expectations while also raising critical questions of fairness, transparency, and the human experience of learning in algorithmically mediated learning systems.

3.2.1 Use of Interactive and Adaptive Learning Resources

Adaptive learning platforms represent a substantial progression from traditional workplace training that offers inflexible course delivery to a more dynamic, individualized path of learning. They monitor a learner's existing level of mastery for skills and concepts, dynamically altering the sequencing and level of difficulty of content, in the moment, to maximize learning pathways. Multiple adaptive platforms utilize concepts from item response theory and recommendation algorithms to decide which modules, exercises, or scenarios will be most useful for the employee to continue developing skill and competency, thus matching the demands of both the organization and the individual needs of the employee.

Interactive learning formats are a feature of many of these systems and can increase engagement and advance knowledge transfer. Microlearning modules, which are often in the 3–12 minute range, generally focus on a single learning outcome and enable employees to develop and reinforce specific skills without cognitive overload. Scenario-based simulations develop branching decision pathways in which learners must navigate experiential learning and reflective practice on the basis of the outcomes of their choices. Engaging and immersive virtual reality (VR) and augmented reality (AR) applications support contextualized, hands-on training to simulate everything from intricate equipment operation and safety procedures to customer interactions and provide opportunities for practice with little to no risk in a high-fidelity simulation. AI-supported practice environments, such as conversational agents, allow learners to role-play interactions—including sales pitches or customer empathy exercises—while receiving real-time, adaptive feedback, thereby fostering deliberate practice and iterative improvement [12].

The educational advantages gained from interactive and adaptive learning tools have been established. Engaging learners in learning activities leads to deeper cognitive processing, supporting retention of information and the ability to transfer knowledge and skills into practice over time. By personalizing the learning path, cognitive overload is reduced because information is provided at the learner's level of optimal challenge, resulting in more effective comprehension and learning satisfaction. Moreover, the immediacy of feedback from a learning tool that uses AI to support learners can accelerate the skill acquisition process since learners can correct errors, consolidate new knowledge and skills, and gain confidence in practice at a rate that is faster than traditional and uniform training and learning experiences. Together, all of the previously described adaptive and interactive learning tools enhance the effectiveness and efficiency of learning and produce a more engaged, skilled, and resilient workforce that is aligned with organizational strategies for workforce development (see Figure 3.1).

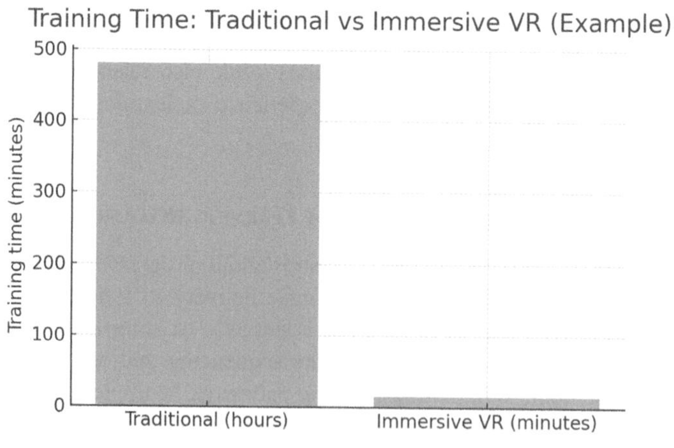

FIGURE 3.1 Training time reduction.

This bar chart illustrates the reduction in training time when immersive learning methods are used compared with traditional approaches. As shown, immersive training can significantly shorten the learning curve, enhancing efficiency while maintaining skill acquisition quality.

3.2.2 Continuous Learning and Skill Development

Continuous learning is changing the approach to training in organizations. It shifts the focus from learning as a series of one-off events to a lifelong habit that is woven into daily work and aligns with both personal career goals and the needs of the organization. Unlike traditional training programs, which often consist of one-time workshops or courses, continuous learning focuses on gradually acquiring skills, obtaining real-time feedback, and adapting. In this way, employees can build their skills in a way that keeps pace with changing job demands and market trends.

At the heart of continuous learning is the development or use of a skills taxonomy or map. This tool connects specific roles to the skills and proficiency levels needed. With a clear skills framework, organizations can pinpoint what skills are necessary for each position, identify gaps in their current workforce, and create targeted strategies for career advancement, whether employees are moving sideways or climbing the ladder [13]. Adding to this structured approach is the idea of learning in the flow of work. This means incorporating bite-sized learning modules, helpful tips, and gentle reminders right into the digital tools that employees use every day—such as Customer Relationship Management (CRM) systems, messaging apps, or productivity software. This method not only makes learning more accessible and relevant but also minimizes interruptions to daily tasks and increases retention through practical, contextual learning.

Career pathways are a vital part of continuous learning initiatives. By outlining both lateral and vertical career moves along with the necessary skill milestones, organizations can offer employees clear development paths and specific learning goals. AI-powered analytics and internal talent marketplaces can enhance this process by pinpointing stretch projects, mentorship opportunities, and role-specific skill-building tasks, creating a rich, personalized development environment.

To keep continuous learning thriving and effective, operational enablers are crucial. Organizations need to set aside budgets for continuous learning and dedicate time, signaling the importance of skill development and encouraging meaningful participation. Support from management is also key: training managers in coaching, giving feedback, and planning development helps employees turn their learning into real performance gains. Finally, internal talent marketplaces—platforms that highlight internal projects, cross-functional roles, and mentorship opportunities—serve as practical tools to bring continuous learning to life, linking employees with hands-on learning experiences that reinforce new skills and broaden their professional networks (Table 3.4).

By weaving these design patterns together with operational enablers, continuous learning programs not only increase skill acquisition and employee engagement but also enhance organizational agility. This ensures that the capabilities of the workforce

TABLE 3.4
Key Design Patterns and Operational Enablers for Continuous Learning

Category	Components	Purpose/Benefits	References
Skills taxonomy	Role-to-competency mapping, proficiency levels	Aligns learning to organizational needs; identifies skill gaps	[14]
Learning in the flow of work	Micromodules, embedded nudges, tool-integrated tips	Increases accessibility, relevance, and retention	[15]
Career pathways	Lateral and vertical career maps, skill milestones	Clarifies development trajectory; motivates engagement	[4, 7]
Operational enablers	Learning budgets, allocated learning time, manager coaching, internal talent marketplaces	Provides resources, support, and practical opportunities for skill development	[15]

evolve in sync with strategic goals. Additionally, AI-driven analytics can keep tabs on skill development, track participation, and identify emerging gaps, allowing for data-informed tweaks to learning initiatives and the thoughtful creation of personalized development paths.

3.2.3 Predictive Analytics for Skill Gaps and Growth

Predictive analytics represents a transformative approach to workforce development, leveraging historical and real-time data to forecast future skill demand, identify current capability gaps, and recommend targeted interventions. By integrating data from multiple organizational and external sources, predictive models provide actionable insights that support strategic workforce planning, succession management, and personalized learning pathways. These systems enable organizations to move from reactive training interventions toward anticipatory, evidence-driven skill development, aligning employee capabilities with both current role requirements and emerging organizational needs.

3.2.3.1 Data Sources for Predictive Models

Effective predictive analytics relies on diverse data sources, each contributing unique insights into workforce capabilities:

1. **LMS Records and Assessment Scores**: Track completion rates, assessment performance, and learning engagement to identify gaps in knowledge and mastery.
2. **Performance Management Ratings and Goals**: These provide longitudinal insight into employee performance relative to expected competencies, highlighting areas of underperformance and development potential.

3. **Project Assignments and Outcomes**: Capture experiential learning, success in cross-functional projects, and applied skill acquisition.
4. **External Labor Market Indicators**: Signal emerging skill demand through job postings, labor platform analytics, and industry trends, enabling organizations to align internal skill development with external workforce trends [9].

3.2.3.2 Typical Predictive Tasks

Predictive analytics in skill development encompasses a range of interrelated tasks that collectively support strategic workforce planning and personalized learning interventions. Skill-gap scoring quantifies the difference between an employee's current proficiency and role expectations, using competency assessments, module completion rates, and other performance indicators to pinpoint specific areas for targeted development [16]. Attrition risk modeling leverages engagement scores, skill mismatch indices, and turnover probabilities to identify employees who may be at risk of leaving, enabling proactive retention strategies and career development support. Finally, succession readiness scoring integrates metrics such as readiness indices, project performance, and mentorship participation to evaluate the preparedness of employees for critical roles, guiding succession planning and prioritizing development resources. Together, these predictive tasks create a data-driven framework that informs both individual learning pathways and broader organizational talent strategies, enhancing workforce capability, engagement, and resilience.

3.2.3.3 Modeling Considerations

While predictive analytics offers significant opportunities, careful attention must be given to ethical, technical, and operational considerations:

- **Fairness and Bias Mitigation**: Models should be transparent about features used and regularly audited to detect disparate impacts across demographic groups [11].
- **Interpretability**: Preference should be given to models that provide actionable guidance, such as explicit recommendations for targeted training ("Skill X proficiency is 40% below role expectation; recommend three modules") rather than opaque probability scores [10].
- **Data Governance and Privacy**: Sensitive attributes must be carefully controlled, consent obtained where needed, and training data secured in accordance with privacy regulations [4].

By integrating predictive analytics with adaptive learning platforms and continuous development programs, organizations can create a closed-loop skill development ecosystem. Insights from predictive models inform the design of personalized learning pathways, guide career progression decisions, and enable proactive interventions to reduce attrition and build organizational capability. This approach not only enhances workforce agility but also ensures that talent development aligns with strategic objectives, employee growth, and evolving market demands [15].

3.2.3.4 Case Study: Immersive and AI-enabled Onboarding at a Large Retailer

A multinational retail company faced long time-to-productivity for store associates handling a new automated fulfillment device (a pickup tower system). Traditional classroom training required device availability and hands-on sessions, which limited throughput.

3.2.3.4.1 Timeline of Implementation

- **Phase 0—Problem Identification (Q1)**: High variance in training outcomes and slow adoption of new technology were flagged in internal audits.
- **Phase 1—Pilot (Q2)**: Partnered with the immersive learning provider STRIVR to develop VR simulations of the pickup tower device. The pilot was launched in ten stores.
- **Phase 2—Scale-Up (Q3)**: Based on pilot success (96% reduction in training time [2]), rollout expanded to 200 stores.
- **Phase 3—Enterprise Integration (Q4)**: Virtual onboarding assistants were integrated into the HR portal, linking VR modules with preboarding tasks.
- **Phase 4—Continuous Improvement (Following Year)**: Analytics dashboards monitored module completion, confidence scores, and retention metrics. Iterative refinements were made to learning pathways.

3.2.3.4.2 Stakeholder Mapping

The success of the immersive and AI-enabled onboarding program relied on careful stakeholder mapping and a structured rollout plan. Executive sponsors, including the Chief Learning Officer and the VP of Operations, provided strategic oversight and ensured alignment with organizational goals. HR and Learning & Development (L&D) teams owned the onboarding workflows, defined key performance indicators, and maintained compliance standards, whereas store managers acted as frontline mentors, offering hands-on guidance and real-time feedback on employee readiness. New hires, as primary beneficiaries, provided crucial input on usability and post-training confidence, helping refine the learning experience. Technology partners, such as STRIVR for VR modules, ServiceNow for virtual onboarding assistants, and the HRIS provider, supplied the technical infrastructure, whereas IT and facilities teams supported headset deployment, network readiness, and the physical setup of VR training spaces.

3.2.3.4.3 Rollout Checklist

The rollout followed a structured checklist to ensure effectiveness and scalability. The process began with a needs assessment to identify high-impact training use cases, such as the pickup tower device, followed by the development of immersive modules aligned with standard operating procedures. Pilot stores received VR hardware kits, and managers were trained to facilitate sessions, ensuring a smooth learning experience. Integration with the HR portal linked VR modules to virtual onboarding assistants, enabling preboarding engagement. Pilot metrics, including time-to-productivity, confidence, and retention, were collected to inform iterative improvements. Content refinement and expanded hardware deployment were accompanied by the establishment of long-term measurement dashboards to monitor ongoing performance.

3.2.3.4.4 Interview-Style Observations

The interview-style observations highlighted the tangible impact of the program. A store manager at a pilot site noted that associates, who previously required days to gain confidence on the pickup tower, were ready within an hour after VR training. New hires emphasized the reduced stress of making mistakes in VR before operating the real machine. An HR program manager noted that the greatest benefit was not just time savings but also standardizing the learning experience across hundreds of stores. Executive sponsors highlighted the combination of AI-enabled onboarding assistants and immersive VR as a driver of both operational efficiency and employee satisfaction.

3.2.3.4.5 Outcomes

The program delivered significant outcomes, including a reduction in training time from several hours to under 30 minutes for core tasks, increased confidence scores among trainees, faster technology rollout across sites, and improved retention rates at 90 days. Key takeaways underscored that immersive simulations can decouple training from physical hardware constraints and that pairing them with automated onboarding assistants enhances both efficiency and engagement. Strong executive sponsorship and IT coordination are critical to scaling these emerging learning technologies. A practical roadmap for implementation involves assessing the current state by mapping onboarding and training processes; defining objectives such as reducing time-to-productivity and increasing retention; prototyping minimal viable onboarding pathways for select roles; integrating systems to ensure data flow between HRISs, LMSs, IT ticketing, and analytics; and scaling with governance frameworks for predictive analytics and continuous measurement.

REFERENCES

1. Bauer, T. N., Bodner, T., Erdogan, B., Truxillo, D. M., & Tucker, J. S. (2007). Newcomer adjustment during organizational socialization: A meta-analytic review of antecedents, outcomes, and methods. *Journal of Applied Psychology*, 92(3), 707–721. https://doi.org/10.1037/0021-9010.92.3.707. PMID: 17484552.
2. Klein, H., Polin, B., & Sutton, K. (2015). Specific onboarding practices for the socialization of new employees. *International Journal of Selection and Assessment*, 23(3), 263–283. https://doi.org/10.1111/ijsa.12113
3. Bondarouk, T., & Brewster, C. (2016). Conceptualizing the future of HRM and technology research. *The International Journal of Human Resource Management*, 27(21), 2652–2671. https://doi.org/10.1080/09585192.2016.1232296
4. Strohmeier, S. (2020). Digital human resource management: A conceptual clarification. *German Journal of Human Resource Management*, 34(3), 345–365. https://doi.org/10.1177/2397002220921131 (Original work published 2020).

5. Allen, D. G. (2006). Do organizational socialization tactics influence newcomer embeddedness and turnover? *Journal of Management*, 32(2), 237–256. https://doi.org/10.1177/0149206305280103 (Original work published 2006).
6. Saks, A. M., & Gruman, J. A. (2011). Getting newcomers engaged: The role of socialization tactics. *Journal of Managerial Psychology*, 26, 383–402.
7. Brynjolfsson, E., & McAfee, A. (2017). *Machine, Platform, Crowd: Harnessing our Digital Future*. W. W. Norton.
8. Campion, M. A., Fink, A. A., Ruggeberg, B. J., Carr, L., Phillips, G. M., & Odman, R. B. (2011). Doing competencies well: Best practices in competency modelling. *Personnel Psychology*, 64(1), 225–262. https://doi.org/10.1111/j.1744-6570.2010.01207.x
9. Huang, M.-H., & Rust, R. T. (2018). Artificial intelligence in service. *Journal of Service Research*, 21(2), 155–172. https://doi.org/10.1177/1094670517752459 (Original work published 2018).
10. Marler, J. H., & Boudreau, J. W. (2016). An evidence-based review of HR analytics. *The International Journal of Human Resource Management*, 28(1), 3–26. https://doi.org/10.1080/09585192.2016.1244699
11. Raghavan, M., Barocas, S., Kleinberg, J., & Levy, K. (2020). Mitigating bias in algorithmic hiring: Evaluating claims and practices. In *Proceedings of the 2020 Conference on Fairness, Accountability, and Transparency (FAT*'20)*, Barcelona, January 2020 (pp. 469–481). Association for Computing Machinery. https://doi.org/10.1145/3351095.3372828
12. VanLehn, K. (2011). The relative effectiveness of human tutoring, intelligent tutoring systems, and other tutoring systems. *Educational Psychologist*, 46(4), 197–221. https://doi.org/10.1080/00461520.2011.611369
13. Majumder, S., & Dey, N. (2024). *The Vogue of Managing People in Workplace* (pp. 1–134). Springer.
14. Cappelli, P. H. (2015). Skill gaps, skill shortages, and skill mismatches: Evidence and arguments for the United States. *ILR Review*, 68(2), 251–290. https://doi.org/10.1177/0019793914564961 (Original work published 2015).
15. Bersin, J. (2018). *Continuous Learning in the Flow of Work*. Deloitte Insights.
16. Bhattacharya, A., Choudhary, P., Mukhopadhyay, S., Misra, B., Chakraborty, S., & Dey, N. (2023). Explainable AI for predictive analytics on employee promotion. In *2023 International Conference on Advanced Computing Technologies and Applications (ICACTA)*, Mumbai, India, October 2023 (pp. 1–7). IEEE.

4 Maximizing Employee Engagement and Retention

Generative artificial intelligence (GenAI; generative AI) can provide significant use cases for businesses in IT, HR, data management, marketing, and customer support, along with various other processes. Generative AI ought to prioritize enhancing the employee experience in the workplace; the aim and basis for adopting new technology should consistently center on establishing human-machine collaboration that fuels innovation. Successful implementation of new technologies will require thoughtful deliberation by the company and its leaders. Understanding the impact of generative AI and implementing a forward-thinking approach allows one to leverage this developing technology to establish a future-oriented workplace where innovation, collaboration, and human-machine synergy flourish, enabling employees to excel.

4.1 PERSONALIZED EMPLOYEE ENGAGEMENT STRATEGIES

Customized employee engagement strategies focus on adjusting engagement initiatives to suit individual employee requirements, preferences, and objectives, instead of applying a universal approach. This involves cultivating a workplace culture in which every employee feels appreciated, engaged, and inspired by linking their tasks to their individual dreams and objectives. Organizations can provide individualized career advancement pathways, health and wellness initiatives, and customized feedback systems. Recognizing the distinct motivations, strengths, and career goals of each employee contributes to a more rewarding work environment. Tailored approaches can enhance the emotional bond between employees and the organization, resulting in higher job satisfaction and loyalty [1]. This can involve providing mentorship tailored to personal career aspirations, offering adaptable work schedules that meet individual requirements, or acknowledging accomplishments in ways that are meaningful to each person. Personalized methods can enhance employee motivation, decrease turnover, and boost overall workplace contentment.

Essentially, personalized employee engagement seeks to establish a workplace where every employee feels recognized, backed, and motivated to give their utmost. This section covers strategies for employee engagement powered by generative AI.

I. **Generative AI in Human Capital Management (HCM)**: Integrating generative AI into HCM is a tactical approach to optimize workflows and improve the overall employee experience [2]. By automating repetitive tasks, HR professionals can shift their attention to strategic initiatives that genuinely

DOI: 10.1201/9781003674887-4

influence organizational growth. Moreover, the customization abilities of generative AI enable HR processes to be adapted to personal requirements, leading to increased employee satisfaction. Moreover, the implementation of data-driven decision-making, enabled by AI-derived insights, allows HR leaders to make knowledgeable decisions that benefit the workforce [3].

II. **Generative AI in Human Resource Management System (HRMS) Transformation**: The evolution of HRMS with generative AI enhances efficiency and precision in data handling. Automating data entry and processing minimizes mistakes while enhancing data accuracy, guaranteeing that HR professionals can access trustworthy information. The incorporation of AI-driven predictive analytics allows organizations to foresee workforce trends, facilitating proactive decision-making that aligns with the changing needs of the workforce.

III. **Generative AI in Talent Management**: Generative AI significantly impacts talent management by enhancing recruitment procedures and supporting skill advancement. The use of AI-based evaluations simplifies candidate evaluation, enhancing the efficiency and effectiveness of the hiring process [4]. Furthermore, generative AI reveals skill deficiencies in the workforce, enabling HR specialists to suggest tailored learning paths for employees. This strategic method not only improves employee growth but also fosters a more capable and flexible workforce.

IV. **Generative AI in Workforce Management**: In workforce management, generative AI aids in enhancing scheduling procedures and delivering important performance insights [5]. Generating effective work schedules that consider employee preferences and business requirements improves scheduling efficiency. Additionally, employing AI to evaluate employee performance delivers practical insights for positive feedback, encouraging ongoing development and employee involvement.

4.1.1 Employee Recognition and Rewards

Acknowledging and rewarding employees is essential for creating a constructive and effective workplace. They recognize employee efforts, inspire excellent performance, and cultivate a feeling of inclusion and gratitude. An employee recognition and rewards program is a structure that acknowledges and compensates the accomplishments and efforts of employees within an organization [6]. Acknowledgment is frequently provided on a platform utilized by internal staff, where points earned through each recognition can be exchanged for rewards. An employee rewards program aims to enhance employee morale, increase performance, and retain talent.

Acknowledging employees greatly influences crucial business metrics such as engagement, productivity, and retention. Developing a meaningful employee recognition and reward system is attainable for any organization, but it demands the appropriate knowledge, preparation, and resources. The aim of an employee rewards and recognition program is to recognize, celebrate, and highlight employee successes and achievements among their co-workers and peers [7].

Workers can receive acknowledgment via social recognition or by earning points that correspond to preferred behaviors. Employees can exchange the points they earn for rewards such as gift cards, products, or experiences. Instances of employee recognition and reward initiatives include i) commemorating employee work anniversaries: acknowledging years of service strengthens dedication and allegiance. A straightforward message, a tailored reward, or a public recognition for achievements such as 1, 5, or 10 years demonstrates to employees that their commitment is valued; ii) organizing employee appreciation events: these events provide chances to honor employees in a significant manner. Team lunches, virtual celebrations, or company-wide gatherings all enhance morale and foster connections. Events that recognize employees and teams for their accomplishments elevate motivation and support company objectives. Acknowledgment during meetings, award ceremonies, or team shout-outs promotes ongoing excellence; iii) weekly or monthly employee highlights: consistent employee highlights emphasize personal achievements and foster a culture of gratitude. Highlighting employees in newsletters, meetings, or social media promotes engagement and appreciation among peers [8].

4.1.2 Preparing Individualized Career Development Plans

Research by the Work Institute revealed that career growth was the primary factor influencing individuals' decisions to remain with or depart from a company. Moreover, 51% of employees believe their organization offers a clear route for career development and promotion. This sharply contrasts with the 90% of employers who consider effective management of career and mobility plans a valuable advantage. The study shows that the absence of a policy for creating distinctive career paths leads to a greater tendency for employees to resign [9]. The variance in perspective regarding the job proposal is attributed to the manager's apprehension about losing the talent. Managers worry that voicing their possible frustrations will exclude them from the "loop." Closing this gap necessitates moving past the emotional aspect of the employee-collaborator relationship.

Personalized Career Development Plans (PCDPs) act as strategic guides designed to help employees achieve their career goals while aligning with organizational needs [10]. Unlike uniform approaches, PCDPs recognize the unique skills, aspirations, and developmental needs of every individual. Creating effective PCDPs requires collaboration between the employee and their supervisor, focusing on self-awareness, goal setting, and actionable steps. Here is a summary of the key steps involved in developing individualized career advancement plans.

I. **Self-Assessment and Reflection**: The process usually starts with the employee contemplating their existing abilities, strengths, and the areas in which they shine. Resources such as self-evaluations, 360-degree assessments, and previous performance reviews can be useful in this context [11]. Grasping what truly captivates and drives the employee is essential for discovering rewarding career avenues. Recognizing the areas in which the employee seeks development or requires enhancement is also essential. This may rely on self-awareness, input, or the demands of their intended career path. What are the employee's immediate and future career objectives? Where do they envision themselves in the upcoming 1–5 years? These become important for this juncture.

II. **Manager-Employee Discussion**: The worker discusses their self-evaluation and professional goals with their supervisor. The manager, in response, shares their views on the employee's performance, potential, and fit with company objectives [12]. They collaborate to investigate possible career trajectories within the organization and converse about prospects for advancement and development. The manager assists in aligning the employee's development goals, when feasible, with the organization's strategic objectives and talent requirements.

III. **Goal Setting (SMART Goals)**: From the self-evaluation, targeted, quantifiable, attainable, pertinent, and time-specific (SMART) objectives are created. These objectives must concentrate on cultivating the essential skills and experiences for the targeted career path, such as i) Specific: clearly articulate what must be accomplished, ii) Measurable: how will advancement be monitored? iii) Achievable: are the objectives practical considering the available resources and timeframe? iv) Relevant: do the aims correspond with the employee's ambitions and organizational requirements? v) Time-bound: what is the deadline for fulfilling each objective?

IV. **Identifying Development Activities**: After establishing goals, the subsequent step is to determine the particular actions and resources required to reach them. These potentially encompass: i) training and workshops: structured educational sessions to gain new expertise and competencies, ii) mentoring and coaching: assistance and advice from knowledgeable mentors, iii) on-the-job experiences: challenging tasks, involvement in projects, or role exchanges to obtain hands-on experience, iv) reading literature, articles, or engaging in online learning, v) networking: establishing connections with industry professionals [13].

V. **Documenting the Plan**: Recording a career development plan involves producing a structured written account of your professional objectives, the actions one will undertake to reach them, and the resources one will require. It serves as a guide for the career path, offering direction, clarity, and a method to monitor one's development. The established objectives, growth activities, and schedules are recorded in an official Individualized Career Development Plan (ICDP). This offers a distinct reference for the manager and the employee. A written plan may be shared with supervisors or mentors for feedback and assistance.

VI. **Regular Review and Follow-up**: ICDPs are dynamic documents. Consistent meetings between the manager and employee are crucial for assessing progress, tackling any difficulties, and modifying the plan as necessary [14]. This guarantees the plan stays pertinent and successful. Advantages of ICDPs include i) higher employee engagement: workers feel appreciated and involved when their growth is emphasized, ii) better retention: offering advancement opportunities can greatly lower employee attrition, iii) improved skills and competencies: ICDPs contribute to a more skilled and proficient workforce, iv) enhanced alignment: personal ambitions can align more effectively with company goals, v) greater motivation: workers are more driven when they perceive a distinct pathway for their career advancement.

Ultimately, crafting PCDPs is an effective approach to promoting employee growth, improving organizational strengths, and fostering a more engaged and dedicated workforce [15]. It demands a dedication to transparent dialogue, shared objective creation, and continuous encouragement for personal ambitions.

4.1.3 Creating Personalized Communication Channels

Generative AI is transforming the landscape of Human Resource Management (HRM) by enabling personalized communication channels that enhance employee engagement, streamline processes, and improve overall organizational efficiency [16]. How this technology is reshaping communication within HRM can be explored by following.

I. **Personalized Employee Interactions**: Generative AI can assess employee data and preferences to customize communication. AI can create customized emails or messages tailored to an employee's position, length of service, and preferences. Smart chatbots deliver immediate answers to employee questions, offering customized assistance suited to personal requirements. AI can assess candidate profiles to formulate job descriptions that appeal to particular demographics. Automated messaging can be custom-made at various points in the hiring process. This improves candidate experience.

II. **Continuous Feedback Mechanisms**: AI can generate personalized surveys based on earlier responses, ensuring that inquiries are relevant to the employee's experiences. The system can evaluate feedback immediately to adjust communication strategies, ensuring that employees feel recognized and valued [17]. AI can create personalized training programs designed to fit an employee's skills, career goals, and learning preferences. Generative AI provides ongoing updates and encouragement to the employee's growth, fostering a supportive learning environment.

III. **Benefits of Personalized Communication**: Incorporating generative AI into HRM communication systems can lead to several benefits. Employees feel a heightened sense of belonging when communications are personalized specifically for them. Personalized communication enhances relationships, leading to improved employee satisfaction and retention. Automating routine communications allows HR professionals to focus on strategic initiatives rather than administrative tasks.

4.1.4 Monitoring and Improving Workplace Culture

Generative AI is being more frequently employed to oversee and enhance workplace culture, providing organizations with creative resources to promote a positive and inclusive atmosphere. Utilizing data analysis, sentiment evaluation, and immediate feedback tools, generative AI can greatly improve comprehension and oversight of workplace interactions. Generative AI can assess employee communications to understand the general sentiment in the organization. AI can analyze extensive amounts of text from emails, chat messages, and feedback forms to detect patterns in employee sentiment [22]. Surveys can be automated to gather employee opinions on their perceptions of workplace culture, enabling rapid evaluations and modifications.

Establishing avenues for prompt feedback is essential for a positive work environment [18]. In automated feedback systems, AI can create instant feedback prompts customized for particular occurrences (e.g., post-team meetings or after project completions). With anonymity options, workers can give truthful feedback without concerns of consequences, fostering a culture of transparency. Generative AI enables organizations to recognize enduring cultural trends by examining past data linked to employee satisfaction, turnover rates, and engagement levels to reveal patterns. By benchmarking internal cultural metrics against industry standards or competitors, areas for enhancement can be pinpointed. AI significantly contributes to advancing diversity and inclusion in the workplace. It can scrutinize hiring and promotion procedures to detect and address biases, promoting equitable practices. From the analysis, AI can recommend targeted programs or initiatives designed to improve diversity and nurture an inclusive atmosphere. Additionally, AI can forecast which teams or departments might face disengagement risks based on historical data and present sentiment [19]. By recognizing possible challenges, HR can apply strategies prior to issues worsening, preserving a favorable workplace atmosphere. Utilizing generative AI to observe and enhance workplace culture presents numerous benefits. By continuously tracking sentiment and feedback, organizations can quickly resolve issues, resulting in better well-being. Enhanced insight into team dynamics can foster collaboration and communication among staff. Insights derived from data empower leaders to make better-informed choices about organizational policies and cultural initiatives.

Generative AI acts as an effective resource for assessing and enhancing workplace culture. By allowing immediate feedback, sentiment assessment, and forecast analytics, organizations can cultivate a more involved, inclusive, and upbeat workplace atmosphere [21]. With the ongoing advancement of AI technology, its influence on workplace culture is poised to grow, aiding organizations in succeeding within a competitive environment [20].

4.2 AI FOR CAREER PROGRESSION AND LEADERSHIP PLANNING

Artificial Intelligence (AI) is transforming the field of career advancement and leadership development in organizations. Utilizing data-informed insights and predictive analysis, AI offers resources that enable workers to manage their professional journeys while helping businesses recognize and develop potential leaders. AI is transforming career advancement and leadership strategies by offering tailored growth opportunities, improving succession planning, and fostering diversity. Through the use of AI-driven insights, organizations can enable employees to steer their career trajectories while maintaining a strong succession of future leaders. As AI technology progresses, its influence on workforce development will grow more substantial, aiding organizations in succeeding within a competitive environment. AI can forecast future leadership requirements by analyzing business objectives, market dynamics, and employee demographics, guaranteeing that organizations maintain a talent pool prepared to assume leadership positions [21]. AI can replicate various scenarios to evaluate how different candidates may excel in leadership roles, aiding organizations in making knowledgeable choices.

4.2.1 Identifying Employee Potential

Generative AI is changing how companies recognize and nurture employee potential through the use of sophisticated data analysis and tailored insights. GenAI can be applied in HR functions by analyzing various data sources—like performance evaluations, project results, and peer assessments—to pinpoint high-potential employees. By identifying trends in performance and accomplishments, it provides a more impartial evaluation of an employee's skills and development path. By assessing personal skills, experiences, and career goals, GenAI can suggest customized learning and development initiatives. This guarantees that employees have access to pertinent training options, promoting ongoing development and involvement. GenAI supports succession planning by pinpointing employees prepared to take on leadership positions. It evaluates elements such as past performance, leadership traits, and flexibility to maintain a strong flow of upcoming leaders. Observing employee sentiment via communication channels enables GenAI to assess morale and levels of engagement [22].

This immediate assessment assists HR in resolving issues quickly, fostering a favorable workplace atmosphere. Through the standardization of evaluation metrics and an emphasis on data-informed insights, GenAI minimizes unconscious bias in recognizing and advancing talent, fostering diversity and inclusion in the workplace. Incorporating GenAI into HR practices allows organizations to make data-driven choices, foster employee growth, and cultivate a robust workforce. Through the standardization of evaluation metrics and an emphasis on data-driven insights, GenAI aids in minimizing unconscious bias in talent identification and advancement choices, fostering diversity and inclusion within the organization. GenAI can predict possible employee attrition by examining trends and behaviors, allowing for proactive retention approaches. This anticipatory method enables HR to take action prior to problems worsening.

4.2.2 AI-Driven Career Path Mapping

AI-powered career path mapping employs machine learning algorithms to evaluate diverse data points—like skills, experiences, performance metrics, and career objectives—to deliver customized career advancement strategies. This technology detects skill deficiencies, proposes training options, and indicates possible career transitions both inside and outside the organization. AI evaluates personal profiles to suggest targeted learning and development initiatives, guaranteeing relevance and efficacy. AI promotes career growth within the organization by identifying appropriate internal opportunities, enhancing employee retention and satisfaction. It identifies gaps between existing skills and those needed for targeted roles, steering focused upskilling initiatives. AI connects employees with mentors whose expertise matches their career goals, encouraging development and knowledge sharing. Organizations can take the initiative to recognize and equip high-potential staff for upcoming leadership positions.

4.2.3 Strategic Leadership Succession Strategies

Generative AI streamlines repetitive tasks, enhancing productivity in the workforce. By freeing employees from repetitive tasks, essential time and resources are shifted to strategic projects, promoting a more effective and vibrant work atmosphere. The incorporation of generative AI provides organizations with data-informed insights, transforming decision-making practices. Leveraging AI-generated data enables organizations to make strategic, informed decisions that align with their objectives, thereby promoting sustainable growth. Optimizing worldwide payroll operations is a key benefit of generative AI. This guarantees adherence across borders while streamlining intricate payroll tasks, lowering the likelihood of mistakes and improving overall payroll precision. The outcome is a payroll system that is more efficient and compliant with global standards. Streamlining tasks with generative AI directly enhances employee satisfaction and involvement.

Eliminating unnecessary complications allows employees to concentrate on meaningful and challenging facets of their jobs, resulting in a more rewarding work experience. Generative AI enables the customization of employee experiences. Customizing HR procedures to meet personal needs helps employees feel acknowledged and appreciated, fostering a positive workplace environment. This individual approach boosts overall involvement and worker commitment. Utilizing generative AI allows businesses to anticipate and tackle problems before they intensify. AI algorithms can identify patterns and irregularities, enabling organizations to implement preventative actions and sustain a healthy, problem-free workplace. Generative AI is not merely a technological progression; it is a transformative factor for employee engagement. By implementing these strategies and utilizing the advantages in exit management, attendance, time management, HCM, HRMS, performance, talent, and workforce management, companies can establish a workplace that is both effective and promotes a culture of engagement and ongoing enhancement.

4.3 CONCLUSIONS

The adoption of generative AI offers a major and revolutionary chance for organizations aiming to enhance employee engagement and retention. Through the automation of repetitive tasks, customization of learning and development, improvement of communication, and delivery of valuable insights regarding employee feelings, generative AI can enable HR management to foster a more supportive, engaging, and personalized workplace. Although the importance of ethical considerations and human oversight is significant, the advantages of utilizing generative AI are certainly clear. By nurturing individual worth through tailored experiences and optimizing workflows to allow human resources to focus on more strategic efforts, generative AI can directly enhance job satisfaction, bolster organizational loyalty, and ultimately improve employee retention rates. With the ongoing evolution of this technology, organizations that thoughtfully embrace and ethically apply generative AI solutions are expected to gain a competitive advantage in attracting and retaining skilled talent, promoting a more engaged and productive workforce, and ultimately achieving greater organizational success. The work landscape, enriched by the smart features of generative AI, offers a more human-focused and immersive experience for workers.

REFERENCES

1. Moore, J. R., & Hanson, W. (2022). Improving leader effectiveness: Impact on employee engagement and retention. *Journal of Management Development*, 41(7/8), 450–468.
2. Chopra, A., Sahoo, C. K., & Patel, G. (2024). Exploring the relationship between employer branding and talent retention: The mediation effect of employee engagement. *International Journal of Organizational Analysis*, 32(4), 702–720.
3. Andari, A., Nafiudin, N., & Purnamasari, R. (2021). The influence of the work environment and employee engagement on employee retention. *Almana: Journal of Manajemen dan Bisnis*, 5(3), 447–453.
4. Ismail, F., Ka, H. K., Fern, N. W., & Imran, M. (2021). Talent management practices, employee engagement, employee retention: empirical evidence from Malaysian SMEs. *Studies of Applied Economics*, 39(10).
5. Bhakuni, S., & Saxena, S. (2023). Exploring the link between training and development, employee engagement and employee retention. *Journal of Business and Management Studies*, 5(1), 173–180.
6. Goyal, R., & Kaur, G. (2023). Determining the role of employee engagement in nurse retention along with the mediation of organizational culture. *Healthcare*, 11(5), 760.
7. Mainali, S. P., & Tantry, A. (2022). Employment retention: Active employee engagement, employee satisfaction and leadership factors of a successful human resource strategic practices in an organization. *Westford Research Journal*, 6(2).
8. Ekhsan, M., Sudiro, A., Mugiono, M., & Hussein, A. S. (2022). Employee retention and change management during times of uncertainty. *Frontiers in Psychology*, 13, 916709.
9. Zainal, N. S. B., Wider, W., Lajuma, S., Ahmad Khadri, M. W. A. B., Taib, N. M., & Joseph, A. (2022). Employee retention in the service industry in Malaysia. *Frontiers in Sociology*, 7, 928951.
10. Yusliza, M. Y., Noor Faezah, J., Ali, N. A., Mohamad Noor, N. M., Ramayah, T., Tanveer, M. I., & Fawehinmi, O. (2021). Effects of supportive work environment on employee retention: The mediating role of person–organisation fit. *Industrial and Commercial Training*, 53(3), 201–216.
11. Ghani, B., Zada, M., Memon, K. R., Ullah, R., Khattak, A., Han, H., … & Araya-Castillo, L. (2022). Challenges and strategies for employee retention in the hospitality industry: A review. *Sustainability*, 14(5), 2885.
12. Allen, D. G., & Vardaman, J. M. (2021). Global talent retention: Understanding employee turnover around the world. In *Global Talent Retention: Understanding Employee Turnover Around the World* (pp. 1–15). Emerald Publishing Limited.
13. Rodprayoon, N., & Maj, S. P. (2021). Workplace diversity influence on employee retention in organizations during the COVID-19. *AU-GSB e-JOURNAL*, 14(2), 130–143.
14. Nayak, S., Jena, D., & Patnaik, S. (2021). Mediation framework connecting knowledge contract, psychological contract, employee retention, and employee satisfaction: An empirical study. *International Journal of Engineering Business Management*, 13, 18479790211004007.

15. Stor, M. (2024). Employee retention and company performance results: The mediating role of HRM outcomes in foreign subsidiaries of Central European MNCs. *Employee Relations: The International Journal*, 46(7), 1422–1445.
16. Almerri, H. S. H. (2023). Investigating the impact of organizational culture on employee retention: Moderating role of employee engagement. *Journal of System and Management Sciences*, 13(4), 488–507.
17. Gelencsér, M., Kőmüves, Z. S., Hollósy-Vadász, G., & Szabó-Szentgróti, G. (2024). Modelling employee retention in small and medium-sized enterprises and large enterprises in a dynamically changing business environment. *International Journal of Organizational Analysis*, 33(5), 1006–1038.
18. Sankari, S., & Geetha, A. (2025). Generative artificial intelligence in employee retention and engagement at IT sectors with reference to Chennai. In *Multidisciplinary Approaches to AI, Data, and Innovation for a Smarter World* (pp. 415–430). IGI Global Scientific Publishing.
19. Nica, E., Szpilko, D., Stamule, S., & Marica, E. M. (2024). Next-generation workforce management solutions: Utilizing generative AI to transform human resource operations, talent acquisition, and employee experience in the digital age. *Psychosociological Issues in Human Resource Management*, 12(1), 50–77.
20. Ahmed, S. (2025). Strategic HRM and generative AI: Case studies on successful implementation of GenAI in SHRM. In *Human Resource Management in the Age of Generative AI* (pp. 47–74). IGI Global Scientific Publishing.
21. Bhattacharya, A., Choudhary, P., Mukhopadhyay, S., Misra, B., Chakraborty, S., & Dey, N. (2023). Explainable AI for predictive analytics on employee promotion. In *2023 International Conference on Advanced Computing Technologies and Applications (ICACTA)*, Mumbai, India, October 2023 (pp. 1–7). IEEE.
22. Khosravy, M., Gupta, N., Pasquali, A., Dey, N., Crespo, R. G., & Witkowski, O. (2023). Human-collaborative artificial intelligence along with social values in industry 5.0: A survey of the state-of-the-art. *IEEE Transactions on Cognitive and Developmental Systems*, 16(1), 165–176.

5 Implementing Generative AI in HR Operations

Generative artificial intelligence (GenAI; generative AI) is swiftly changing multiple sectors, including human resources (HR). This innovative technology, able to generate new content like text, images, and code, offers a unique chance to transform conventional HR functions by automating repetitive activities, improving decision-making, customizing employee experiences, and encouraging innovation. Generative AI can greatly boost efficiency, precision, and strategic influence within the HR department. This introduction examines the transformative impact of generative AI on HR, detailing its possible applications, advantages, and the factors required for effective implementation in today's work environment.

5.1 PREPARING YOUR BUSINESS FOR AI ADOPTION

In November 2022, ChatGPT changed the globe. This was developed and is maintained by OpenAI. The chatbot introduced users to a relatively novel concept: AI-driven content generation. In just two months, the application attracted over 100 million users. A little over two years later, generative AI has permeated almost all industries [1]. The manner in which the technology functions is surprisingly simple. It starts with a particular AI model that has been trained on billions, and occasionally even trillions, of data points. Over time, the model starts to recognize semantic patterns within its training data, which it can subsequently use to generate content. Naturally, large language models (LLMs) like ChatGPT are the most well-known examples, generating text based on user questions. In that same context, there are also GenAI models for images, videos, audio, and coding. Besides content generation, GenAI can be used for predictive analysis, data handling, and automation. In 2023, Samsung encountered numerous data breaches, which included internal meeting notes, design documents, and source code—all because it allowed its staff to utilize ChatGPT [2]. The semiconductor giant failed to understand that, like numerous consumer GenAI tools, OpenAI's software evolves based on user interactions. Later that year, Samsung, along with several other companies, restricted their employees' use of generative AI. The issue was not with the GenAI technology itself. It involved the use of consumer software in a corporate setting. Most free AI tools are not designed with security or compliance considerations; instead, they focus mainly on ease of use and accessibility. Sharing sensitive or proprietary information on these platforms can lead to problems. Besides security issues, consumer GenAI tools typically adopt a standardized method [3]. They cannot be tailored for a specific

DOI: 10.1201/9781003674887-5

application or use case, nor are they designed to integrate with enterprise systems and software. They frequently struggle with terminology specific to the industry and lack comprehension of a business's operational framework. In simpler terms, while appropriate for general questions and nonsensitive tasks, consumer GenAI falls short in more specialized or complex fields.

5.1.1 Myths About AI Technology in HR

"Myths about AI Technology in HR" refers to common misconceptions, baseless beliefs, or exaggerated claims concerning the capabilities, impact, and incorporation of AI within the HR field. These myths typically stem from a misinterpretation of the technology, fears of job displacement, or unrealistic expectations [4]. They could hinder the adoption of beneficial AI tools or lead to their misuse. Numerous common themes in these myths include: i) AI will entirely replace HR professionals, ii) AI is inherently biased and leads to unfair outcomes, iii) AI lacks the "human touch" necessary for HR activities like employee engagement, iv) AI is too expensive or too complicated for most HR departments to implement, v) AI can make completely impartial decisions. Understanding and debunking these misconceptions is crucial for HR professionals to effectively evaluate and implement AI technologies, thus enhancing their positions and providing strategic advantages to their organizations.

Many common misconceptions exist about AI in HR, including the idea that AI will replace HR jobs, that its only advantage is in recruitment, and that it is too complex for numerous organizations. Nevertheless, AI primarily supports HR professionals by streamlining tasks and providing data-driven insights, allowing them to focus on strategic initiatives and employee relations. AI will replace HR jobs [5]. AI will render HR roles unnecessary, leading to considerable reductions in employment. AI improves the capabilities of HR professionals, allowing them to focus on essential tasks like talent development and employee engagement. AI can handle repetitive duties like reviewing resumes and coordinating schedules, enabling HR professionals to concentrate on strategic goals. Although AI can streamline candidate prescreening, human recruiters are vital for assessing cultural fit and building connections. The primary application of AI in HR is limited to hiring and evaluating candidates [6].

AI's impact extends beyond recruitment, offering essential insights into workforce engagement, talent development, and even sales and marketing strategies. Predictive analytics can identify employees at risk of leaving, allowing HR to take preventive actions. Implementing AI solutions is excessively challenging and complex for numerous organizations [7]. Chatbots powered by AI can handle routine employee questions, reducing the workload on HR and allowing them to focus on more complex issues. AI tools can provide instant solutions to HR challenges and generate optimal outcomes. Even though AI can suggest potential candidates, human recruiters still need to assess their cultural fit and suitability for the role. Establishing AI solutions is a fast and easy process. Careful selection of AI solutions is essential, and it is important to ensure they align with organizational needs before putting them into action.

As AI advancements continue to transform sectors, HR remains no exception. By utilizing advancements like AI-powered hiring, labor analytics, and automated staff communication platforms, many companies are adopting AI to improve their HR processes. However, despite its rapid implementation, persistent misunderstandings about AI in HR often lead to hesitations about its use. This section discusses the misconceptions related to AI [8].

I. **AI Will Replace HR Professionals**: A widespread belief is that AI will render HR professionals obsolete. AI tools are designed to assist HR professionals instead of replacing them. AI has the ability to handle monotonous and repetitive tasks, such as the initial candidate assessment, coordinating interviews, or filtering through large volumes of data. This allows HR professionals to focus on their main strengths: nurturing talent, fostering company culture, and advancing strategic initiatives. AI applications, for example, can sift through many resumes to find the best candidates according to specific criteria; however, they still require human input to assess cultural fit or connect with potential applicants. AI enhances the capabilities of HR professionals by providing practical insights and enabling them to concentrate on high-value activities that demand human intuition.

II. **AI Is Too Expensive for Most HR Departments**: Many small to medium-sized businesses (SMBs) steer clear of AI, thinking it is only affordable for large companies. Even though implementing AI technologies might entail upfront costs, the benefits and savings over time often significantly outweigh the initial investment. AI in HR can significantly lower hiring costs, improve employee retention, and increase operational efficiency. Integrass Tech Solutions offers personalized AI solutions that scale according to the needs and size of the organization. Affordable choices for smaller businesses mean that investing in AI does not have to be expensive. AI-driven HR solutions can quickly showcase their Return on Investment (ROI) by reducing hiring durations, decreasing turnover rates, and improving employee satisfaction.

III. **AI Can't Be Trusted to Make Fair Hiring Decisions**: Hiring bias is a significant concern, and many believe that AI will simply perpetuate or exacerbate this issue. However, when used correctly, AI can genuinely help minimize bias. Human recruiters might inadvertently apply their biases in the hiring process, while AI systems, when properly trained, can evaluate candidates solely based on skills, experience, and qualifications without personal bias [9]. Nonetheless, it is essential to develop AI algorithms responsibly. AI tools must be created with diverse datasets and regularly assessed to ensure they remain fair and unbiased. Integrass can work alongside to create a customized AI solution for HR team that adheres to ethical AI principles, fostering fairness and inclusivity in hiring process.

IV. **AI Is Too Complicated for HR Teams to Implement**: Many think that using AI requires advanced technical skills, which can intimidate HR teams. Still, many AI applications are designed to be user-friendly and approachable, serving those without technical backgrounds as well. AI solutions tailored for HR generally feature intuitive, drag-and-drop interfaces or automated reporting tools that enable straightforward implementation. Integrass Tech Solutions specializes in developing AI solutions that effortlessly integrate into existing

HR processes. This offers hands-on training and support to ensure that HR team is confident using these tools right from day one. The team of experts will work to ensure a smooth transition and ongoing success.

V. **AI Lacks the Human Touch Needed for Employee Engagement**: A different misunderstanding is that AI is unable to address the personal and emotional aspects of HR, such as employee engagement and satisfaction. While AI cannot substitute for human interaction, it can enhance the way HR professionals engage with employees. AI-powered platforms can reliably monitor employee satisfaction, detect potential issues, and suggest customized solutions to sustain high engagement levels. For instance, AI can provide tailored surveys based on employee performance data or predict when an employee might be nearing burnout. This allows HR professionals to intervene with effective solutions before problems escalate [10]. Leveraging Integrass' AI tools allows to implement a forward-thinking approach to employee engagement, helping address concerns instantly and maintain a motivated and satisfied workforce.

VI. **AI Only Works for Large Corporations**: Many individuals believe that AI is only suitable for Fortune 500 companies or large technology firms. Nevertheless, AI tools can be customized to fulfill the needs of organizations of any scale, covering various industries. Whether a startup or a long-standing business, AI can help streamline HR processes, improve hiring strategies, and increase employee retention rates. At Integrass, every organization is distinct. This is the reason this offers tailored AI solutions specifically created for distinct HR needs, regardless of a company's size [11]. If an individual needs help automating hiring process or leveraging workforce analytics, AI can positively influence the outcome.

VII. **AI Will Result in Data Security Threats**: With the increasing use of AI, there are worries that these technologies could endanger sensitive employee data to cybersecurity risks. However, AI systems can truly enhance data security by utilizing advanced encryption methods and automated monitoring tools that detect breaches more rapidly than traditional methods.

The illustration of AI in HR is provided here. AI technologies are changing the HR industry, but they also bring a range of myths and misunderstandings. The reality is that AI enhances the skills of HR experts, reduces costs, and can be implemented easily, regardless of the company's scale. If executed correctly, AI can help promote fairness in hiring, enhance employee engagement, and improve data security. At Integrass, organizations develop AI solutions tailored to their specific HR needs. It should be optimizing hiring processes, improving employee engagement, or evaluating workforce data [4].

5.1.2 Assessing HR Needs

Assessing HR requirements entails a systematic method to identify and evaluate an organization's current HR needs and abilities, while also identifying gaps between the necessary resources and those that exist at present. This approach helps organizations align their HR strategies with business goals, prioritize HR activities, and allocate resources efficiently. It fundamentally requires understanding the current state of HR and determining what is needed to achieve organizational objectives. Generative AI has the potential to enhance content creation (including job postings, training materials, employee correspondence, etc.). It can also provide quick access to relevant information through chatbots or knowledge bases. Additionally, generative AI has the ability to tailor employee communications or learning experiences for onboarding materials, policy updates, or internal announcements. Generative AI primarily focuses on content creation, but it can also extend to summarizing and presenting data at times. In this context, "Assessing HR Requirements" ensures that the use of generative AI is strategic and focused on solving genuine HR issues and delivering true value, instead of simply adopting the technology for its own sake. It helps align the capabilities of generative AI with the specific requirements and objectives of the HR function [12].

5.1.3 Establishing a Complete AI Strategy

Developing a thorough AI strategy requires implementing a structured approach that connects AI initiatives with the overall business goals. A summary of the key steps involved is as follows:

I. **Define AI Vision and Objectives**: In this section, understanding the organization's strategic objectives and identifying how AI can help achieve them are discussed. Prioritize the business needs before delving into technology. For example, if a company's objective is to enhance customer experience, a related AI goal could be to implement AI-powered chatbots for customer support. Detail goals regarding what one hopes to achieve with AI. This vision must be communicated across the organization to guarantee unity. One can establish clear, measurable, achievable, relevant, and time-bound (SMART) goals for AI initiatives, for example, reduction of customer support response time by 20% within 6 months using AI chatbots.

II. **Assess Current State and Readiness**: It is crucial to evaluate the existing data resources in terms of their quality, availability, and governance. AI performs best with high-quality data, so comprehending the data landscape is crucial. Assess current IT infrastructure to determine its capability for managing AI tasks. Consider the demand for cloud services, high-performance computing, and specialized technology. Evaluate the AI competencies within the organization. Identify any deficiencies in knowledge concerning data science, machine learning engineering, and AI ethics. Evaluate whether there is a necessity to improve the capabilities of existing staff or to hire new personnel. Review past AI initiatives and their outcomes to assess the organization's current level of AI integration.

III. **Identify High-Potential AI Use Cases**: Examine business operations to identify areas where AI can automate functions, deliver insights, improve decision-making, or enhance customer experiences. Evaluate possible uses based on their potential worth and feasibility. Focus on affordable, high-impact projects for quick wins. Consider the alignment with strategic objectives and the potential return on investment. For each prioritized use case, clearly define the problem intended to be resolved, the anticipated outcome, and the criteria that will be used to evaluate success [13].

IV. **Develop a Data Strategy and Governance Framework**: Data strategy involves defining the methods for gathering, storing, managing, and using data for AI projects. Guarantee data integrity, protection, and availability. Data governance involves creating policies and processes for overseeing data assets, which encompass data privacy, security, and adherence to regulations.

V. **Design AI Operating Model**: Generative AI can change organizations by enabling the creation of innovative applications that enhance experiences for customers and employees alike. Organizations are utilizing generative AI in production for diverse applications, such as intelligent document processing, translation and summarization, personalized responses for customer support representatives, bespoke marketing content, along with image and code creation. Big corporations often have different business units that run several lines of business (LOBs), overseen by a central governance body, and typically utilize AWS Organizations in conjunction with an Amazon Web Services (AWS) multi-account strategy [14]. They establish landing zones to automate the secure account creation process and streamline account management, integrating logging, monitoring, and auditing. While LOBs manage their individual accounts and tasks, a central team such as the Cloud Center of Excellence (CCoE) supervises identity, regulations, and access protocols.

With the ongoing expansion of generative AI, organizations need to create an operational framework for it. An operating model outlines the organization's framework, essential processes, technologies, roles and obligations, governance structures, and financial arrangements that sustain a business's operations.

VI. **Operating Model Patterns**: Organizations can adopt different operating models for generative AI, depending on their priorities related to agility, governance, and centralized management. Governance in generative AI involves the frameworks, rules, and processes that enable the responsible development, deployment, and use of these technologies. It comprises several approaches aimed at minimizing risks, improving accountability, and ensuring that generative AI systems align with ethical principles and organizational objectives. The three common patterns of operating models are decentralized, centralized, and federated, as illustrated in the following diagram.

a) **Decentralized Model**: In a decentralized model, individual LOBs initiate and oversee the development and deployment of generative AI. LOBs maintain control over their AI processes, models, and data within their specific AWS accounts. This allows for quicker time-to-market and flexibility since LOBs can swiftly test and implement generative AI solutions customized to their requirements. Nevertheless, even within a decentralized framework, LOBs frequently need to synchronize with central governance controls and secure approvals from the CCoE team for production deployment, following global enterprise standards

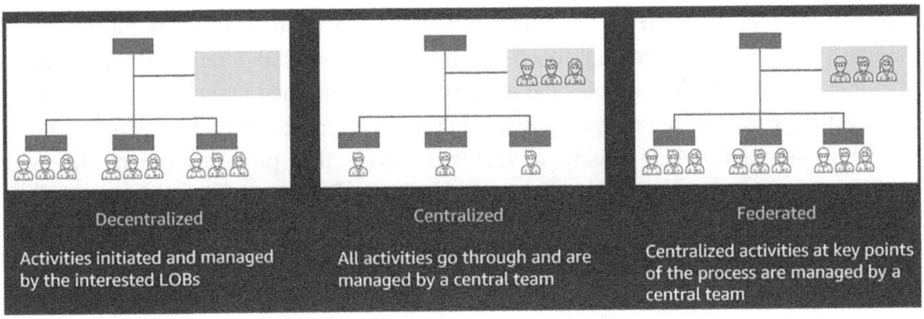

FIGURE 5.1 Operating model patterns.

concerning aspects like access policies, model risk management, data privacy, and compliance posture, which may complicate governance (see Figure 5.1).

b) **Centralized Model**: In a centralized operational model, a core team focused on generative AI and machine learning (AI/ML) manages all generative AI tasks, supervising and coordinating extensive AI workflows, models, and data across the organization [15, 16]. LOBs collaborate with the central team for their AI needs, trading off agility and potentially longer time-to-market for improved top-down supervision. A centralized model can lead to bottlenecks that delay time-to-market, so organizations need to adequately staff the team and implement automated processes to efficiently manage the demands from various LOBs. The lack of team expansion can weaken the governance benefits of a centralized approach.

c) **Federated Model**: A federated model reaches a balance by having essential functions of the generative AI processes managed by a central team dedicated to generative AI/ML platforms. While LOBs drive their AI initiatives, the central team monitors guardrails, manages model risk, ensures data privacy, and upholds compliance. This enables quick LOB innovation while maintaining centralized oversight of governance matters [17].

5.2 GENERATIVE AI ARCHITECTURE COMPONENTS

Before delving deeper into the common operating model patterns, this section offers a brief overview of various components and AWS services employed in the noted architectures.

Extensive machine learning models, known as LLMs, contain billions of parameters and are pretrained on significant data sets. LLMs may encounter hallucinations, meaning that a model can provide a confident but incorrect response. Moreover, the data the model was trained on might be old, leading to incorrect responses. One approach to lower the likelihood of LLMs giving incorrect information is through a strategy known as Retrieval Augmented Generation (RAG). RAG is an advanced natural language processing approach that combines knowledge retrieval with generative text models. RAG combines the advantages of pretrained language models with a retrieval approach to generate responses that are more accurate and knowledgeable.

To implement RAG, having a vector database that provides the model with pertinent source documents is essential. Utilizing RAG, relevant document fragments or additional texts are sourced and supplied to LLMs to generate targeted answers with enhanced quality and relevance. Amazon Bedrock is a fully managed service offering a variety of high-performance foundation models (FMs) from leading AI firms such as AI21 Labs, Anthropic, Cohere, Meta, Mistral AI, Stability AI, and Amazon via a single API, along with numerous features necessary for developing generative AI applications while upholding security, privacy, and responsible AI practices. Amazon SageMaker JumpStart provides access to unique FMs from external vendors such as AI21 Labs, Cohere, and LightOn. Moreover, Amazon SageMaker JumpStart incorporates and oversees open source FMs from third-party providers such as Hugging Face [18].

5.2.1 Create an AI Strategy Roadmap and Implementation Plan

An AI strategy roadmap is a comprehensive outline that details a business's approach to implementing AI technology. It serves as a strategy, detailing the steps an organization will take to integrate AI into its operations, products, and services. The transformative capabilities of AI technologies are a key focus for every business leader; however, it is the Chief Information Officer (CIO) who is always accountable for turning the concept of AI into real business value. A structured AI roadmap has therefore become crucial for CIOs and other AI leaders who must manage and prioritize the various tasks necessary for successful AI implementation. The Gartner AI Roadmap tool helps plan and progress the critical activities required for large-scale AI implementation in an organization. It assigns key responsibilities to seven workstreams, enabling leaders to select and organize those that most closely.

5.2.2 Choose the Right AI Tools and Technologies

Choosing suitable AI tools and technologies for generative AI implementation requires careful consideration of various factors. It is not just about selecting the most favored tool, but instead about finding the perfect fit for specific requirements and goals. This includes evaluating the tool's features, ease of use, compatibility with existing systems, and potential ethical implications.

5.2.3 Focus on Adoption and Change Management

"Highlighting Adoption and Change Management in Generative AI" recognizes that technology implementation is only one part of the complete picture. The human element—how people adapt to and utilize these new tools—is equally important, if not more so, for realizing the full potential of generative AI within an organization. Without this focus, even the most sophisticated generative AI tools may not be utilized optimally, leading to diminished returns on investment and missed chances [19].

5.2.4 Measure, Monitor, and Iterate

"Evaluate, Monitor, and Improve" creates a feedback loop essential for the ongoing success of AI strategy. It ensures that AI initiatives are active, continuously evolving and improving, delivering increasing value to the organization over time. This iterative approach allows organizations to learn from executions, adapt to changing conditions, and maximize the advantages of AI investments.

5.3 ADDRESSING ETHICAL AND REGULATORY CONSIDERATIONS

Generative AI, while powerful, can introduce new risks and challenges that HR teams need to handle carefully. Generative AI models learn from datasets, and if those datasets contain biases (like historical biases in hiring data), the AI might perpetuate or exacerbate these biases in its outputs, leading to unfair or discriminatory outcomes in areas such as candidate reviews, performance evaluations, or educational resources. Using generative AI often involves dealing with confidential data regarding employees or candidates. HR must ensure compliance with data privacy regulations (including General Data Protection Regulation (GDPR), Central Consumer Protection Authority (CCPA), and India's DPDP Act) related to collecting, using, and storing this information. This entails being transparent with individuals about how their data is utilized by AI. Understanding how a generative AI model produces a particular result can be challenging. In HR, especially concerning choices that impact individuals (like promotion recommendations), a level of transparency and clarity is crucial to ensure fairness and build trust. It is crucial to establish accountability when an AI system makes a mistake or produces a biased outcome. Clear responsibilities need to be established.

The rise of AI in HR may lead to concerns among HR professionals about their jobs. Ethical considerations involve managing this transition thoughtfully, perhaps through retraining or redefining roles. When generative AI creates content (like training materials or job descriptions), challenges related to ownership and intellectual property rights may arise. HR needs to ensure that the implementation of generative AI complies with all applicable employment laws and regulations, which could evolve as AI utilization grows.

5.3.1 Choosing and Integrating AI Solutions

"Choosing and Integrating AI Solutions in HR Systems" is very similar to "Choosing and Integrating AI Solutions in HRM Operations." The slight difference centers on the system itself, indicating a priority on how AI tools fit into the technological structure used by HR. Here is an examination taking that subtlety into account: i) assess existing HR technology framework: understand the advantages and drawbacks of current Human Resource Information System (HRIS), talent management systems, and other HR tech tools. Discover ways for AI to enhance these systems, ii) point out system-wide challenges: where are there inefficiencies, data silos, or lack of intelligent automation in current HR systems? iii) describe improvements via AI:

detail how AI could upgrade HR systems, such as smart workflows, automated data handling, or better user interfaces, iv) stress compatibility: prioritize AI solutions that offer robust APIs or seamless integration capabilities with existing HR systems, v) evaluate integration approaches: understand how the AI solution will connect (e.g., direct API link, middleware). Consider the technical complexities and maintenance needed. Ensure the AI solution can safely and effectively access and manage the critical data from HR systems. Numerous HR system vendors are increasingly integrating AI directly into their platforms. Evaluate if these combined features meet needs [20, 21].

Examples of AI integration in HR systems: to address HR questions directly on the platform. Algorithms in machine learning embedded within the HRIS: to analyze employee information for insights regarding turnover risk or skill gaps, shown directly on the system's dashboards. AI-driven talent acquisition tools in the Application Tracking System (ATS): for automated evaluation and alignment of candidates integrated into the recruitment process. NLP-enabled tools embedded in performance management systems: to analyze feedback and provide more comprehensive performance evaluations within the platform. The key difference is the focus on how AI functions as an integral part of the HR tech ecosystem, enhancing the intelligence and automation capabilities of the tools that HR professionals use regularly. This requires careful consideration of technical compatibility and data transfer in the HR technology ecosystem.

5.3.2 Evaluating AI Tools and Vendors

Evaluating AI tools and vendors requires a systematic approach, highlighting essential elements like data transparency, compliance, efficiency, and support. It is crucial to understand the vendor's expertise, their technology integration, and their ability to scale and merge with existing systems.

I. **Clarify Objectives**: The first step is to define clear goals for an AI project and specify exactly what the organization aims for this tool to achieve. One should ideally pinpoint a specific problem they want to tackle; however, it must also reflect on, "Is this genuinely an AI application or merely a use case?" One can subsequently evaluate whether AI might be a fitting option. One may discover that AI is not required.
II. **Analyze the Provider**: Once an AI solution that seems like a good fit is discovered, it is essential to assess the companies behind the tools prior to proceeding. Is one feeling compelled by conventional suppliers to implement an AI solution that works with their current technology? Is there a startup that centers its efforts on a specific AI application one is engaged with? If it is the latter, consider aspects such as their duration of existence, sources of funding, and whether they seem like an organization that can be trusted regarding the data. A more thorough security evaluation should be conducted later in the assessment process, but addressing this now can assist in eliminating inappropriate providers.

III. **Study Customer Use Cases**: Identify the total number of customers currently served by the tool providers, as well as the number of those who are paying customers. Obtain present use cases and engage in dialogues with customer references. Individuals ought to engage with the people who are actually using the tool.

IV. **Is the Tool Industry Specific?**: Individuals have been highly impressed by, industry-specific tools that are emerging in areas such as manufacturing, marketing, architecture, engineering, and construction. These tools are designed to address the unique needs of these industries and their particular data formats. A 3D CAD model is not exactly the same as a spreadsheet. Industries often have regulations that pertain only to their activities as well. A specialized tool designed for a specific industry that addresses a particular need can be very advantageous.

V. **Ensure the Tool Will Scale**: Regardless of all this, the tool must continue to grow. Architecture firms and marketing agencies are among the largest clients of many AI vendors. They manage large amounts of file data and many international sites and studios. A small provider that has developed a solution with the right technical infrastructure may handle enterprise-level functions—or it might face challenges when growing [22].

VI. **Gauge the Complexity**: A technical evaluation should help to gauge the challenges of execution and usage. Determine whether further education is required for staff.

VII. **Check for Bias and Regulatory Adherence**: It is important to understand if the vendor has assessed their solution for bias in the training data and what measures have been implemented to protect against data breaches or unauthorized access to their system. AI regulations are continually changing around the world, making it crucial to ensure that the tool complies with the regulations relevant to the sector and geographical locations.

VIII. **Evaluate Transparency**: How thoroughly is transparency incorporated into the model when it reaches conclusions? Ideally, a specific degree of clarity is desired. If the model proposes an idea that is disagreeable or conflicts with principles, individuals need to understand the reasoning behind it and adjust the response to prevent repeating the same mistake.

IX. **Define Success in Advance**: The criteria for evaluating success upon completion of this project must be defined clearly from the beginning. By choosing to integrate an AI chatbot into customer service tools, for instance, one might aim to reduce customer support requests by 10%–15%. This metric can be set beforehand with the solution provider to ensure that the goal is attainable and meaningful.

X. **Map Out the Cost**: The overall expense of implementing an AI solution relies on several responses provided earlier. People have to specify the expenses for implementation and maintenance, including whether extra personnel are necessary, and so forth. Ideally, the provider people select ought to offer ROI forecasts, accompanied by verified case studies or client stories illustrating practical implementations [23].

5.3.3 Integration with Existing HR Systems

Incorporating generative AI into current HR systems requires comprehension of the AI's features, selecting suitable tools, and modifying HR processes to include the new capabilities. This integration may result in considerable enhancements in efficiency, data analysis, and employee engagement; nonetheless, it necessitates a phased approach, involving pilot testing, training, and ongoing optimization. AI is an innovative and transformative technology that allows machines to imitate human skills like understanding, reasoning, learning, and making decisions. By utilizing sophisticated algorithms and examining large datasets, AI has the ability to automate intricate tasks, provide tailored solutions, and revolutionize multiple industries by enhancing efficiency and fostering innovation. Currently, leading corporations like Google, Microsoft, and IBM are investigating AI. Its uses are varied, and it can be easily incorporated into HR.

Until 2017, AI had a minimal presence in the HR sector in France. That changed at the VivaTech trade fair that year, where various startups began leveraging AI to improve HR processes. An increasing portion of repetitive jobs could be managed by "machines" that are capable of functioning independently [24]. This pertains to recruitment, particularly when the process of interviewing and selecting the right candidate can be exhausting for the recruiter. Nonetheless, that is not all. At present, AI in HR covers the entire range of the employee experience, including recruitment, exit, training, skill development, and mobility. HR can utilize AI to improve and optimize its overall approach.

5.4 GENERATIVE AI FOR HR

Generative AI refers to a category of AI methods that create new content, including images, text, audio, and videos, derived from input data or models learned from training datasets. For HR, generative AI involves using generative AI methods in managing HR. Generative AI can be utilized in various manners within HR, such as customized learning and training, skills evaluation and enhancement, talent sourcing and hiring, as well as employee involvement and feedback. Incorporating generative AI into current HR systems necessitates a careful and technical strategy to guarantee smooth functioning and data integration. The following is an overview of the essential actions.

I. **Identify Use Cases and Integration Points**: Improve the development of job descriptions, training resources, policy revisions, and employee messaging. Improve search functionalities in HR systems for documents, FAQs, and knowledge repositories. Customize educational resources, onboarding documents, or messages according to specific employee information. Integrate chatbots within HR systems to respond to employee questions. Identify the systems (such as HRIS, Learning Management System (LMS), ATS, employee portals) that would gain the greatest advantage from generative AI features.
II. **Evaluate Generative AI Solutions and Integration Capabilities**: Investigate alternatives that correspond with specified use cases. Identify ways in

which these tools can integrate with current HR systems. Typical approaches comprise: numerous contemporary software systems provide APIs that facilitate communication and data exchange among various applications. Automatic alerts dispatched from one application to another upon the occurrence of specific events. Resources and offerings that facilitate integration. Enable the AI to access information straight from the HR system's database. Assess the technical requirements for integration and the continual upkeep [25].

III. **Plan the Integration Process**: Illustrate the flow of data between HR systems and the generative AI tool. Evaluate data formats and required transformations. Confirm that the integration complies with data privacy laws and the organization's security procedures. Record the elements that are part of the integration and how they relate to each other. Set up the AI platform based on requirements. Employ APIs, webhooks, or alternative approaches to link the AI with HR systems. This typically includes development tasks. Make sure the generative AI model thoroughly understands data from HR systems and that the reverse is true as well.

IV. **Test and Validate**: Confirm that the integration functions as intended, data are transferred accurately, and the generative AI generates the expected outcomes within the HR system framework. Engage HR experts in the testing stage to confirm the unified solution fulfills their requirements. Allow HR staff to access the system. Monitor the application of generative AI and its effects on HR procedures. Get ready to address and solve any issues that come up. Integration examples: merging a generative AI chatbot with an HR portal: through APIs, the chatbot can access HR knowledge resources and employee information to respond to questions directly in the portal. Linking a generative AI content creation solution to an LMS: using APIs, the AI can autonomously generate training modules or quizzes that are subsequently uploaded to the LMS. Integrating generative AI into an ATS: through APIs, the AI can autonomously create initial outreach emails to candidates using job descriptions and candidate profiles saved in the ATS.

Effective incorporation of generative AI into current HR systems necessitates teamwork among HR, IT, and possibly outside vendors. A comprehensive grasp of requirements, the characteristics of generative AI, and the framework of existing systems is essential for seamless and efficient integration [26].

5.4.1 Ensuring Data Security and Compliance

In 2024, the landscape of data security compliance has expanded and diversified, profoundly influenced by worldwide digital transformation and a heightened emphasis on data privacy. Legislation like the GDPR in the EU, the CCPA in the US, and comparable laws globally have set rigorous criteria for privacy and data security. The International Association of Privacy Professionals (IAPP) provides a comprehensive resource hub featuring information on international data privacy regulations (https://iapp.org/). This may act as a crucial resource for analyzing the current compliance landscape. Key compliance challenges for businesses include: global disparity in regulations: navigating the extensive range of local and international data protection regulations remains a significant challenge for multinational corporations. Technological adaptation: keeping up with rapidly evolving technology and ensuring that compliance tools are up to date is a continual struggle. Data complexity: the swift growth in the diversity of data types and sources has made data mapping and classification more complicated, obstructing compliance efforts.

The partnership between AI and data security compliance in 2024 highlights advancements in technology and strategic foresight. AI has transformed from an innovative tool into an essential component for ensuring compliance. According to International Data Corporation (IDC) forecasts, by 2024, data classification tools powered by AI will automate 70% of activities associated with the classification of Personally Identifiable Information (PII).

AI systems efficiently enhance the categorization, management, and storage of data while ensuring compliance with regulations like GDPR and CCPA. AI-powered tools permit immediate monitoring of data streams, quickly detecting any compliance breaches and providing detailed reports for regulatory agencies. Through predictive analytics, AI anticipates future compliance needs, allowing businesses to stay aligned with regulatory changes. A worldwide banking organization implemented an AI system that independently modifies its data storage techniques to comply with evolving global financial regulations. This system reduced manual work and significantly lessened the likelihood of noncompliance. A healthcare worker employed AI to manage patient data. The AI system ensured HIPAA adherence while identifying potential data breaches, enhancing overall data protection [27].

5.4.2 Preparing Your Team for Transformation

As organizations strive to integrate generative AI into their processes, preparing the team for this transition is crucial. This involves understanding the technology, adjusting workflows, enhancing skills, and fostering a culture that encourages innovation. Here is a comprehensive approach to effectively prepare the team for the generative AI shift. Generative AI involves algorithms that can produce original content, such as text, images, or music, based on the data utilized for training. Tools like ChatGPT and various LLMs exemplify generative AI, proficient in producing human-like writing and assisting with numerous tasks in different fields. Generative AI is set to transform business landscapes by automating tasks, enhancing creativity, and improving decision-making processes. Acknowledging its potential impacts is essential for teams to effectively use these tools.

5.4.3 Guiding HR Teams on AI Technologies

Generative AI refers to algorithms that can create original content such as text, images, or music, based on the data they were trained with. Tools like ChatGPT and other LLMs are prominent examples of generative AI, capable of producing text that resembles human writing and assisting in various tasks across numerous industries. Domain experts and product managers are essential as they understand user needs and can effectively communicate the goals that the AI needs to fulfill [1]. Their expertise in prompt engineering—developing clear instructions for AI—will be vital for successful implementation. Multifaceted engineers capable of managing both front-end and back-end development are increasingly important. They can integrate AI features into existing systems without needing in-depth machine learning expertise.

Emerging roles like “AI Engineer” seek to bridge traditional engineering with AI capabilities, enabling teams to quickly adapt to changing technologies. Training team members in prompt engineering is vital. This skill involves delivering accurate and context-rich instructions for AI models, which can significantly impact the quality of AI outputs. Workshops and hands-on sessions can help team members refine and enhance their prompt engineering skills. Nurturing a culture of continuous learning is essential as AI technologies evolve rapidly. Encourage team members to stay updated on the latest advancements in generative AI through online courses, webinars, and industry gatherings. This proactive approach will help the team adapt to changes and use new tools effectively.

5.4.4 Addressing Resistance to Change

Implementing generative AI within a corporate environment may encounter resistance for various reasons, including fears of job displacement, lack of understanding, disruptions to workflows, and concerns regarding ethics. To effectively address this resistance, a thorough approach highlighting communication, education, and involvement is crucial. Here is a summary of strategies**: i) understand the roots of resistance**: conduct surveys, organize discussions, and listen to staff to grasp their individual and collective worries about GenAI. Recognize that resistance is a typical human response to change and address worries with empathy, **ii) communicate information clearly and transparently**: clearly articulate the reasons for implementing GenAI, highlighting its benefits for the organization and potentially for employees (e.g., easing monotonous tasks, encouraging creativity). Explain what GenAI is expected to achieve and what it will refrain from doing within the organization. Emphasize that it often acts as a way to improve human capabilities instead of entirely replacing them. If specific roles are expected to change, confront the matter openly and present plans for retraining or repositioning staff. Keep in touch with staff throughout the implementation stage by providing updates and addressing any new questions that arise, **iii) teach and train**: provide accessible training and materials to help employees understand the basics of GenAI, including its potential and constraints. Highlight the chances for employees to gain new skills and work alongside AI, improving their positions and career progression. Provide training customized for distinct roles and the impact of GenAI on everyday tasks. Spot early adopters and motivate them to share their favorable experiences and support their peers, **iv) involve employees in the process**: involve employees in identifying possible uses for GenAI and in assessing and enhancing AI solutions. This creates a sense of ownership. Create groups consisting of people from different departments to collaborate on AI implementation, ensuring a variety of perspectives are represented. Start with minor pilot initiatives to demonstrate the benefits of GenAI and build assurance before wider implementation, **v) address ethical concerns**: develop ethical guidelines for AI use, emphasizing data privacy, bias, and accountability. Guarantee clarity concerning the ethical principles guiding the implementation of GenAI within the organization, and **vi) highlight successes and provide support**: recognize and applaud effective GenAI applications to inspire excitement and showcase its positive outcomes. Provide resources and support systems to help employees adapt to new tools and processes [28, 29].

In summary, addressing resistance to change while implementing GenAI requires a proactive and people-centered approach. Through fostering understanding, providing transparency, and involving employees in the process, organizations can improve acceptance and unlock the transformative potential of GenAI.

5.4.5 Fostering a Culture of Continuous Improvement and Learning

To promote a culture of ongoing growth and learning, leaders must exemplify the behaviors they want to inspire, cultivate a secure and nurturing atmosphere, encourage transparent communication, and offer chances for education and advancement. Concentrate on enabling employees, acknowledging achievements, and actively soliciting feedback to consistently refine procedures and improve results.

Continuous improvement identifies opportunities to reduce waste and streamline processes. Overall, it aims to find opportunities to conduct processes more effectively and produce better outcomes with reduced resources (see Figure 5.2). Though this approach originated in manufacturing, continuous improvement is essential for

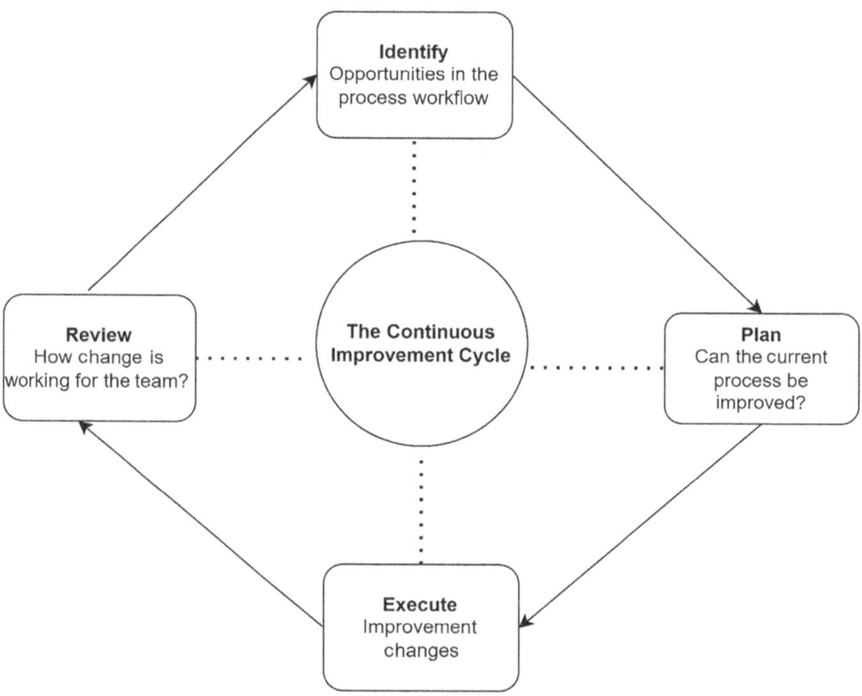

FIGURE 5.2 Cultural improvement and learning.

many successful companies across different industries. For many people, there is no doubt that encouraging continuous improvement can result in enduring, long-lasting effects. The more crucial question frequently concerns whether it can be effectively executed across all levels of the organization.

Employees, as part of an organization, can encourage and support continuous improvement while simultaneously benefiting from it. Employees, as members of an organization, can contribute to and support continual improvement while also enjoying its benefits.

The Kaizen method is almost identical to this approach. The term translates to "ongoing enhancement" in Japanese. Popularized by Toyota, Kaizen focuses on making small, consistent improvements to existing processes, relevant at every organizational tier. Kaizen challenges the entrenched "this is how we've always done it" attitudes often found in established organizations. By making minor adjustments, Kaizen eliminates waste and obstacles. It aims to create consistent processes in product quality, business activities, and compliance with optimal practices such as resource expenses, delivery schedules, non-value-adding tasks, attitude management, training, workflow, documentation, and safe work conditions. An ongoing improvement culture is essential as it brings together effective leadership practices, upgrade methods, and enabling technologies into a significant push for iterative lean approaches [30]. Continuous improvement initiatives distinctly refine processes, elevate product quality, and boost productivity by producing greater output with identical resources. Active leadership is arguably the most essential element for attaining success in promoting a culture of continuous, sustainable enhancement. Organizations driven by leaders who emphasize employee involvement and supportive technology, while consistently utilizing a systematic improvement process, succeed in nurturing a culture focused on ongoing enhancement.

Engaged leadership may be the crucial element for attaining success in nurturing a culture of continuous, sustainable improvement.

I. **Lead by Example**: One must show dedication to a culture of continuous improvement by fully embracing lean management and best practice principles. Participate in continuous improvement initiatives energetically and openly. Act on ideas and motivate others to do the same. Track progress, tackle any issues, and celebrate successes [31]. The team needs to observe commitment to a culture of continuous improvement before they can be expected to embrace that culture independently.
II. **Communicate Regularly**: One should build support in the organization by sharing the benefits and importance of continuous improvement with all stakeholders whenever feasible. Consistent, regular communication during this period is also essential for fostering the appropriate mindset in employees—a significant hurdle in creating a culture of ongoing enhancement. A growth mindset that promotes ongoing learning will lead to lasting enhancements. Think about holding coaching and training sessions that promote new behaviors and develop necessary skills, like efficient problem-solving.

III. **Request Suggestions for Enhancements**: Employees want to feel valued; they seek to know that their opinions matter. Moreover, frontline employees are typically most capable of identifying process or systemic issues, so seek their input for improvements and respond quickly to their recommendations. Nonetheless, avoid merely asking for ideas that directly influence profits or meet a particular ROI target. By cultivating an environment where all improvement ideas are welcomed, employees will encourage both innovation and accountability.

IV. **Empower Employees**: Empower staff to incorporate continuous enhancement into their daily responsibilities. Encourage them, supply continuous improvement tools, knowledge, and time required to assess their current methods, allowing them to regularly identify opportunities for betterment. Once an improvement is implemented, ask employees to document this change, making it the norm for the future—until further improvement opportunities present themselves [32].

V. **Emphasize the Importance of Small, Incremental Improvements**: Refrain from considering each improvement as an event or project, since this approach does not sustainably promote a culture of ongoing enhancement. Rather, encourage small, incremental improvements in all positions and at every tier of the organization. These improvements, known as Kaizen, are vital and create the basis for a culture of continuous, sustainable advancement as every employee engages in the enhancement efforts.

VI. **Help Share Ideas and Improvements**: Share continuous improvement ideas and updates via emails, newsletters, bulletin boards, or any other available platform. The effectiveness of a continuous improvement culture relies on its successful integration throughout the organization, with full participation and responsibility for advancements from all members. Creative ideas, improvements in individual or group performance, and Performance Improvement Plan (PIP) savings shared and easily accessible through visual management—like on digital dashboards for teams—will boost team involvement, motivation, and morale.

VII. **Celebrate the Results Achieved Through Continuous Improvement**: Recognize accomplishments by formally (and informally) celebrating the teams and individuals responsible for the progress. Ongoing recognition boosts employee engagement and motivates other teams and members to improve their processes as well. Create incentives via a reward and recognition framework that appreciates every achievement in ongoing enhancement.

VIII. **Encourage Participation by Keeping the Methodology Simple**: Organizations that thrive in fostering a culture of ongoing enhancement succeed because of their simple approach. Streamline the enhancement strategy to guarantee that all can participate and identify opportunities for growth.

In an organization that has successfully achieved cultural transformation, ongoing enhancement assumes a significant position [33]. This is because all staff and leaders in the organization acknowledge that progression is a vital aspect of their responsibilities, and they approach it with the same seriousness and diligence as they do any other essential performance measure.

5.5 CONCLUSIONS

The integration of generative AI into HR operations signifies a significant leap forward, offering the potential to transform how organizations hire, manage, and develop their employees. This chapter has explored the different applications of GenAI across the HR lifecycle, such as automating recruitment processes, personalizing learning experiences, enhancing employee communication, and generating insightful data analysis. The benefits of implementing GenAI in HR are substantial, including increased efficiency, improved experiences for candidates and employees, data-driven decision-making, and allowing HR professionals to focus on more strategic and human-oriented tasks. However, successful implementation encounters numerous challenges. As stated, organizations must carefully consider ethical implications, data privacy concerns, the importance of robust data infrastructure, and the need to address potential resistance from staff. By thoughtfully tackling these elements, organizations can utilize generative AI to improve the efficiency, engagement, and effectiveness of their HR operations, resulting in a stronger and more successful workforce. The future of HR is increasingly intertwining with AI, and those who carefully embrace this technological advancement will be ready to thrive in the evolving landscape of talent management.

REFERENCES

1. Aguinis, H., Beltran, J. R., & Cope, A. (2024). How to use generative AI as a human resource management assistant. *Organizational Dynamics*, 53(1), 101029.
2. Ahmed, S. (2025). Strategic HRM and generative AI: Case studies on successful implementation of GenAI in SHRM. In *Human Resource Management in the Age of Generative AI* (pp. 47–74). IGI Global Scientific Publishing.
3. Rane, N. (2024). Role and challenges of ChatGPT, Gemini, and similar generative artificial intelligence in human resource management. *Studies in Economics and Business Relations*, 5(1), 11–23.
4. Ardichvili, A., Dirani, K., Jabarkhail, S., El Mansour, W., & Aboulhosn, S. (2024). Using generative AI in human resource development: An applied research study. *Human Resource Development International*, 27(3), 388–409.
5. Chowdhury, S., Budhwar, P., & Wood, G. (2024). Generative artificial intelligence in business: towards a strategic human resource management framework. *British Journal of Management*, 35(4), 1680–1691.
6. Nica, E., Szpilko, D., Stamule, S., & Marcia, E. M. (2024). Next-generation workforce management solutions: Utilizing generative AI to transform human resource operations, talent acquisition, and employee experience in the digital age. *Psychosociological Issues in Human Resource Management*, 12(1), 50–77.
7. Majumder, S., & Peng, S. L. (2024). Artificial intelligence and decent work: Balancing efficiency with human-centric values. In *International Conference on Advances in Information Communication Technology & Computing*, Shymkent City, Kazakhstan, April 2024 (pp. 1–13). Springer Nature Singapore.
8. Abdelhay, S., Haider, S., Hazaimeh, H. M., El-Bannany, M., & Marie, A. (2024). The impact of generative AI (ChatGPT) on the HR functions related hiring process. In *Artificial Intelligence, Digitalization and Regulation* (pp. 369–383). Springer.
9. Gowrishankkar, V., Shanmugam, V., Muhammed, A. A., Sanjeevan, B., Veerachamy, R., & Maheswaran, M. (2025). Human resource management in the epoch of generative AI: Opportunities and challenges. In *Advancements in Intelligent Process Automation* (pp. 51–78). IGI Global.

10. Majumder, S., & Dey, N. (2022). Artificial intelligence and knowledge management. In *AI-empowered Knowledge Management* (pp. 85–100). Springer Singapore.
11. Ajaero, O., & Anjorin, J. B. (2024). Human resource management and generative artificial intelligence (ChatGPT): Nexus, perspectives and praxis. *Global Journal of Human Resource Management*, 12(5), 19–29.
12. Masrek, M. N., Anuar, M. A. W., & Mazlan, N. H. Harnessing generative AI in human resources: A strategic approach to cost reduction and workforce optimization. *International Journal of Research and Innovation in Social Science*, IX(I), 2343–2355.
13. Brink, D. (2024). *Exploring changes: The role of generative AI in transformations in the work of HR generalists* (Master's thesis). University of Twente.
14. Selim, N., Abdelhay, S., Hassan, D., & El-Bannany, D. M. (2024). The impact of generative AI (ChatGPT) on recruitment efficiency and candidate quality: The mediating role of process automation level and the moderating role of organizational size. *Frontiers in Human Dynamics*, 6. Available at SSRN 5150225.
15. Singh, L., Randhelia, A., Jain, A., & Choudhary, A. K. (2025). Ethical and regulatory compliance challenges of generative AI in human resources. In *Generative Artificial Intelligence in Finance: Large Language Models, Interfaces, and Industry Use Cases to Transform Accounting and Finance Processes* (pp. 199–214). Wiley.
16. Mauri, M., Tamma, C., & Corso, M. (2025, February 6). Artificial intelligence and human resources: innovative trends and main impacts. https://hdl.handle.net/10589/231575
17. Abdelhay, S., AlTalay, M. S. R., Selim, N., Altamimi, A. A., Hassan, D., El-Bannany, M., & Marie, A. (2025). The impact of generative AI (ChatGPT) on recruitment efficiency and candidate quality: The mediating role of process automation level and the moderating role of organizational size. *Frontiers in Human Dynamics*, 6, 1487671.
18. Das, S., Chakraborty, S., Sajjan, G., Majumder, S., Dey, N., & Tavares, J. M. R. (2022). Explainable AI for predictive analytics on employee attrition. In *International Conference on Soft Computing and Its Engineering Applications*, Anand, India, December 2022 (pp. 147–157). Springer Nature Switzerland.
19. Venugopal, M., Madhavan, V., Prasad, R., & Raman, R. (2024). Transformative AI in human resource management: Enhancing workforce planning with topic modeling. *Cogent Business & Management*, 11(1), 2432550.
20. Majumder, S., & Mondal, A. (2021). Are chatbots really useful for human resource management?. *International Journal of Speech Technology*, 24(4), 969–977.
21. Kaakandikar, R., Gawande, R. P., Deshmukh, V. A., Raskar, S., & Mulani, H. I. (2024). The strategic significance of artificial intelligence (AI) in HR operations and management. *European Economic Letters (EEL)*, 14(3), 1424–1433.
22. Yang, Y. (2022). Artificial intelligence-based organizational human resource management and operation system. *Frontiers in Psychology*, 13, 962291.
23. Devi, K., Singh, J., Garg, N., Tiwari, M., Shaik, N., & Elangovan, M. (2024). Measuring AI′s impact on HR strategies and operational effectiveness in the era of industry 4.0. In *International Conference on Innovation and Emerging Trends in Computing and Information Technologies*, Punjab, India, March 2024 (pp. 97–107). Springer Nature Switzerland.
24. Ghosh, S., Majumder, S., & Peng, S. L. (2023). An empirical study on adoption of artificial intelligence in human resource management. In *Artificial Intelligence Techniques in Human Resource Management* (pp. 29–85). Apple Academic Press.
25. Joshi, S. (2025). Generative AI in business: Visual illustrations of applications and insights from Q1 2025. http://dx.doi.org/10.2139/ssrn.5237428
26. Majumder, S., Chowdhury, S., Dey, N., & Santosh, K. C. (2022). Balance your work-life: personal interactive web-interface. *International Journal of Interactive Multimedia and Artificial Intelligence*, 7(7), 90–96.

27. Semujanga, B., & Mikalef, P. (2024). Theorizing generative AI in strategic human resource management. In *AMCIS 2024 Proceedings*, Salt Lake City, UT, August 2024 (p. 19). Association for Information Systems.
28. Gupta, H., & Kaur, J. (2025). Optimizing HR operations with generative AI: A strategic healthcare approach. In *Generative AI for Business Analytics and Strategic Decision Making in Service Industry* (pp. 195–218). IGI Global Scientific Publishing.
29. Majumder, S., & Dey, N. (2022). Tools for knowledge management. In *AI-empowered Knowledge Management* (pp. 17–36). Springer Singapore.
30. Kobbacy, K. A., & Vadera, S. (2011). A survey of AI in operations management from 2005 to 2009. *Journal of Manufacturing Technology Management*, 22(6), 706–733.
31. Walter, H. (2024). Streamlining HR operations: The role of microservices in workforce management. *Implementation Science*, 19, 27. https://doi.org/10.1186/s13012-024-01357-9
32. Heijden, L. M. A. (2019). *Classification-based approach for question answering systems: Design and application in HR operations* (Master's thesis). University of Twente.
33. Reddy, S. (2024). Generative AI in healthcare: an implementation science informed translational path on application, integration and governance. *Implementation Science*, 19(1), 27.

6 Navigating Ethical and Legal Frontiers

Privacy, Bias, and Compliance

6.1 INTRODUCTION

In the swiftly changing digital environment of today, the convergence of ethics and law creates a complicated terrain that organizations need to approach cautiously. As data become increasingly essential to decision-making, ethical considerations related to their collection, utilization, and management have gained prominence. Privacy, bias, and compliance are essential elements of this conversation, influencing how organizations and enterprises function in a data-centric landscape. Privacy concerns have increased as people have become more cognizant of their rights related to personal information [1]. The introduction of laws such as the General Data Protection Regulation (GDPR) and the California Consumer Privacy Act (CCPA) highlights the importance for organizations to focus on ethical data management. These rules not only require adherence but also promote a culture of openness and responsibility in managing data. Additionally, the problem of bias in data-driven technologies, especially in artificial intelligence and machine learning, poses important ethical dilemmas. As algorithms play a greater role in making decisions related to hiring, lending, and law enforcement, the risk of systemic bias may result in unjust outcomes that disproportionately impact marginalized groups. Confronting these biases is not just a legal duty but a moral necessity that organizations need to address to promote fair practices. Ultimately, adhering to ethical standards and legal guidelines is essential for building trust with stakeholders. Organizations that implement strong ethical standards not only reduce risks linked to data misuse but also improve their reputation and promote lasting connections with customers [2]. As we explore the difficulties and tactics for addressing these ethical and legal boundaries, it becomes evident that a proactive stance is essential for ensuring that data practices reflect societal values and personal rights.

6.2 ETHICAL CONCERNS IN GENERATIVE AI FOR HR

With the evolution of generative AI technologies transforming the HR landscape, numerous ethical issues arise that organizations need to address. Incorporating AI into HR functions—from hiring and assessing performance to fostering employee involvement—offers potential for efficiency and creativity but also presents major

DOI: 10.1201/9781003674887-6

concerns regarding privacy, bias, and responsibility. Employing generative AI in HR can improve decision-making and optimize processes, but it also presents risks concerning data security and the chance of reinforcing current biases. For example, recruitment tools powered by AI might unintentionally prefer certain demographics, resulting in biased hiring practices. Likewise, AI-driven performance evaluation systems may mirror past inequities, leading to biased evaluations that damage employee morale and trust. Additionally, the regulatory environment is changing quickly, with frameworks such as the EU AI Act imposing strict standards for AI application in HR. These rules seek to safeguard individual rights while also urging organizations to embrace responsible AI practices that emphasize fairness and transparency. HR professionals must balance the advantages of AI against its ethical considerations, ensuring that technology enhances workplace equity instead of obstructing it [3].

6.2.1 Bias and Discrimination in AI-Generated Recommendations

Bias in AI models generally originates from two factors: the model design and the training data utilized. Models can occasionally mirror the beliefs of the developers who program them, leading to a bias toward specific results. Moreover, AI bias can arise from the data utilized to train the AI. AI models operate by examining extensive collections of training data through a method called machine learning. These models recognize trends and relationships within these data to generate forecasts and choices. When AI algorithms identify historical biases or systemic inequalities present in their training data, the results they produce may also mirror those biases and inequalities. Owing to the large-scale data processing capabilities of machine learning tools, minor biases in the initial training data can result in widespread discriminatory effects. This article explores the origins of AI bias, its real-world manifestations, and the importance of addressing AI bias. Bias and discrimination in AI-driven recommendations are critical concerns that emerge when artificial intelligence systems are employed to influence decisions impacting individuals and communities. These prejudices can appear in different ways, frequently resulting in unequal treatment due to race, gender, or other demographic factors. As organizations more frequently depend on AI for decision-making tasks—such as hiring, promotions, and performance assessments—the likelihood of these biases affecting results raises considerable issues [4, 5]. Bias in AI can stem from various phases of the AI development process. A key source is data gathering; if the training data lack diversity or representation, the AI system might generate biased suggestions. An AI developed using historical hiring data that include mainly male candidates might prioritize male applicants in subsequent hiring choices, reinforcing gender bias. Moreover, data labeling can lead to bias since human annotators might unintentionally impose their own biases while categorizing data. Various forms of bias can influence AI-generated suggestions. Selection bias occurs when the training data fail to represent the wider population accurately, resulting in biased outcomes. For example, facial recognition systems predominantly trained on lighter-skinned people might have difficulty accurately recognizing individuals with darker skin tones.

Confirmation bias may also contribute, as AI systems can strengthen existing biases by prioritizing patterns that match past data, such as favoring candidates from demographics that have been historically successful. The consequences of biased AI recommendations can be significant. Unfair hiring practices can result in limited diversity within the workplace, whereas biased performance assessments can reduce opportunities for marginalized groups. Additionally, these biases can undermine trust in AI systems since people might feel unjustly evaluated or left out due to erroneous algorithms. In this section, mitigation strategies are discussed [6]. Tackling bias in AI-generated suggestions necessitates a comprehensive approach. Organizations can utilize varied and representative training datasets to guarantee that AI systems gain insights from a broad array of viewpoints. Moreover, utilizing bias detection tools and performing regular audits can assist in recognizing and correcting biases in AI systems. Promoting transparency in AI decision-making is essential, as it enables users to grasp how suggestions are formed and to contest potentially biased results. Although AI-generated suggestions offer the potential to improve efficiency and impartiality in decision-making, it is crucial to remain alert to the biases that may emerge. By actively addressing these issues, organizations can aim to develop more just and equitable AI systems that serve all people.

6.2.2 The Impact of AI-Driven Decisions on Workplace Diversity and Inclusion

The growing use of AI in workplace decision-making, especially in terms of recruitment, performance assessment, and promotions, offers both advantages and obstacles for diversity and inclusion. Although AI algorithms can reduce unconscious human biases through the use of objective standards, their success depends on the quality and representativeness of the data used for training. When historical data showcase current societal biases or are lacking in diversity, AI systems may unintentionally reinforce or even intensify these biases, resulting in discriminatory results and obstructing attempts to foster an inclusive workforce. On the other hand, carefully crafted and consistently supervised AI systems, developed with varied data collection methods and ethical principles, can uncover unseen talent sources, increase fair chances, and nurture a genuinely diverse and inclusive work environment. AI-informed choices can greatly influence workplace diversity and inclusion, presenting both benefits and obstacles. Although AI can assist in recognizing and reducing bias in hiring and advancement procedures, which may result in a more varied workforce, it also poses the danger of reinforcing current disparities if not thoughtfully developed and applied. AI-driven tools can examine large datasets to detect patterns of bias and offer insights for developing more inclusive policies and practices [7, 8].

Nevertheless, if the information utilized to train these algorithms mirrors existing societal prejudices, the AI might unintentionally uphold those biases in its choices, resulting in inequitable outcomes for specific groups. As a result, organizations need to focus on transparency, accountability, and human oversight during the creation and implementation of AI systems to guarantee that they support DEI objectives and foster an authentically inclusive work environment. The potential of AI for diversity and inclusion is extremely significant now, considering the emphasis on developing diverse and inclusive work environments. An effective diversity strategy entails utilizing equal opportunity as a means for organizational growth, resulting in enhanced problem-solving capabilities, innovation, and employee contentment. A varied workforce allows management to address issues in a more innovative way, resulting in a stronger and more imaginative organization. As AI becomes increasingly integrated into HR processes, it has the potential to reduce biases and inequalities, assisting organizations in achieving their Diversity and Inclusion goals. This study explores the beneficial effects of AI on the transformation of HR practices to promote diversity and inclusion. It explores how AI can be used to remove traditional biases and enhance processes such as recruitment, evaluation, and training. Additionally, the study offers suggestions for implementing AI to create improved and more varied work environments while maintaining ethical principles and standards [9, 10]. This work will utilize a literature review and case analyses to demonstrate how AI can enhance diversity and inclusion within HR. The results will be beneficial for HR practitioners to comprehend how AI can assist in fostering an inclusive organizational culture.

6.2.3 Benefits of AI for Workforce Diversity and Inclusion

AI's role in workforce diversity and inclusion: AI technology holds significant promise for enhancing D&I conditions in the workforce. When strategically designed and efficiently integrated into HR functions, AI can serve as a powerful tool to combat misunderstandings in employee recruitment or advancement, improve data analysis methods, and yield superior outcomes for equitable decision-making. This section outlines the primary use of AI in achieving D&I goals and enhancing policies to address workplace inequalities.

Figure 6.1 illustrates the idea of diversity, equity, inclusion, and belonging (DEIB) within organizations and depicts how these components are linked to foster a positive workplace environment. Diversity fundamentally signifies the acceptance and representation of various aspects of individuals, whereas equity guarantees that

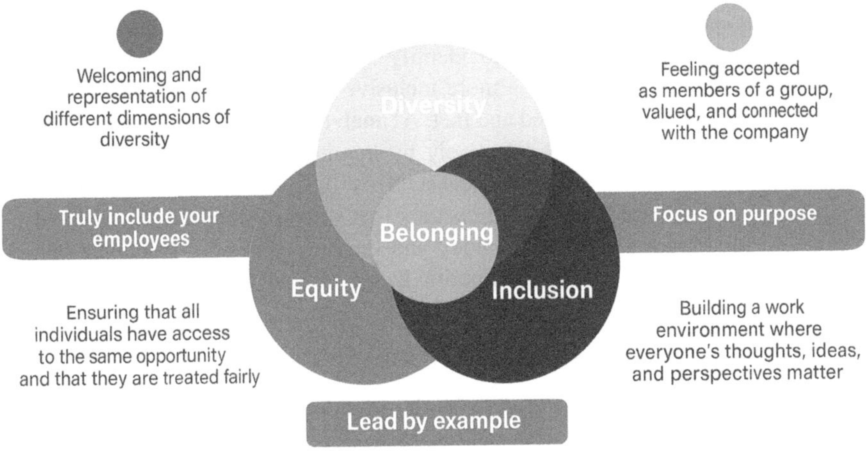

FIGURE 6.1 DEIB in the organization.

all individuals have the same access to opportunities and are treated justly. Inclusion focuses on establishing a workplace where every voice, idea, and perspective is appreciated, whereas belonging signifies that employees feel accepted, valued, and linked to the organization. The DEIB framework is grounded in guiding principles such as accountability, setting a good example, making deliberate efforts, prioritizing purpose, and guaranteeing that inclusion reaches gig workers as well. The diagram collectively emphasizes that DEIB is more than just a collection of policies; it serves as a cornerstone for promoting equity, representation, and unity within organizations.

Artificial intelligence (AI) is increasingly acknowledged as a powerful catalyst for promoting workforce diversity and inclusion (D&I). Its advantages cover various aspects of organizational functions, including hiring, staff development, and workplace culture, contributing to the establishment of fairer and inclusive settings. Tools powered by AI can greatly minimize the unconscious biases that frequently affect hiring choices. AI encourages merit-based selection by evaluating candidates on their skills, qualifications, and potential instead of their demographic traits [11]. Tools such as Textio enhance job postings to employ inclusive language, drawing on a wider and more varied group of candidates. AI can anonymize applications and identify biased language in job descriptions, promoting more equitable hiring practices. This results in a broader range of talent recruitment and encourages an inclusive company culture.

AI imparts impartiality to decision-making by examining extensive datasets to identify trends of bias or discrimination in promotions, compensation, and employee treatment. Predictive analytics can detect disparities early, enabling organizations to take proactive measures. This helps guarantee fair opportunities and treatment for all employee groups, minimizing systemic inequalities. AI-powered learning platforms customize training and development programs to suit individual employee needs, preferences, and learning styles. This customization guarantees that every employee, irrespective of their background, can access pertinent development opportunities. Programs for coaching and mentorship driven by AI offer continuous assistance, aiding in bridging development gaps and encouraging career growth for marginalized groups. AI advancements improve workplace access for disabled individuals with innovations such as text-to-speech, speech-to-text, and gesture recognition. Furthermore, AI tools assess employee wellness by examining communication trends and work habits to identify stress or burnout, allowing prompt assistance. These abilities foster a more inclusive and supportive workplace where different needs are acknowledged and met. AI analytics allow organizations to assess diversity and inclusion results effectively by monitoring employee demographics, promotion rates, and engagement levels. This data-oriented method assists in pinpointing improvement areas and ensures that organizations are responsible for their D&I objectives [12]. Transparency and ongoing oversight guarantee that AI systems do not reinforce biases, promoting trust and equity.

6.3 ETHICAL DILEMMAS IN AUTOMATION

Ethical issues in automation primarily center on concerns regarding bias, transparency, accountability, and employment loss, as well as apprehensions about privacy, security, and the potential for AI technologies to be misused. These concerns arise as automated systems, particularly AI-driven systems, become more prevalent across various sectors of life, such as hiring, healthcare, and military functions. Automation, which involves the use of technology, software, processes, or robotics to perform tasks with minimal human intervention, is transforming industries and societies worldwide. While automation offers significant benefits in terms of efficiency, productivity, and innovation, it also poses various ethical dilemmas that require careful evaluation and responsible management. Key ethical challenges associated with automation can be analyzed through real-life instances, research findings, and proposed ethical frameworks.

6.3.1 Job Loss and Workforce Disruption

A significant ethical concern is the substitution of human workers with automated systems. Predictions suggest that up to 800 million jobs could be eliminated globally by 2030, affecting both low-skilled and high-skilled sectors [13]. This move may lead to increased income inequality, social discord, and mental health issues among affected workers. Automation frequently benefits highly skilled employees and those who own or manage technology, potentially widening the gap between the rich and the poor. This polarization may result in a shrinking middle class and heightened social and political turmoil. Businesses have a moral obligation to assess the impact of automation on their workforce [13]. Ethical approaches include providing retraining, skill development, and support programs for employees impacted by layoffs, as seen with the shutdown of Nokia's plant in Germany.

6.3.2 Bias, Fairness, and Discrimination

Automated systems, especially those powered by AI, can perpetuate and even amplify the biases present in their training data. Amazon's AI hiring tool allegedly favored male candidates because of biased historical data, raising concerns about fairness and discrimination in automated decisions. The "black box" nature of many AI systems makes it difficult to comprehend their decision-making processes, which may conceal biases and hinder efforts to ensure fairness. This lack of clarity is particularly troubling in vital areas such as hiring, funding, and legal systems [14].

6.3.3 Accountability and Responsibility

With increased reliance on machines for decision-making, attributing responsibility becomes challenging when problems occur. The Uber self-driving car event in Arizona, resulting in pedestrian fatality, highlighted the difficulties of accountability in autonomous technology. A collaborative accountability model that involves developers, operators, and business leaders is often proposed. However, this may diminish individual responsibility and make it more difficult to attribute fault to any one entity for negative outcomes. Integrating ethical standards during the design and execution of automated systems is essential to ensure that they operate within acceptable legal and ethical boundaries.

6.3.4 Privacy, Surveillance, and Data Collection

Automated systems often rely on large-scale data collection, resulting in significant privacy concerns. Using personal data without adequate consent or transparency can lead to privacy violations, as seen in targeted advertising and healthcare applications. AI-driven surveillance systems could infringe on personal autonomy and lead to extensive monitoring, facilitating potential abuse by governments or corporations. These systems might adversely impact marginalized groups more because of biased algorithms. Effective data collection and use require robust governance systems, privacy-centric technologies, and adherence to regulations, such as the General Data Protection Regulation (GDPR).

6.3.5 Safety, Security, and Human Well-being

Automated systems, especially in critical areas such as transportation and healthcare, may pose safety risks if they are not properly designed, tested, or monitored. The deployment of lethal autonomous weapons in the military raises substantial ethical issues related to delegating life-and-death decisions to machines [15]. Continuous ethical discussion emphasizes the importance of involving humans in essential decisions, particularly as systems become more autonomous and intricate.

6.3.6 Societal and Global Impacts

The rapid progression of automation may lead to societal disruption, causing changes in jobs, community structures, and possibly cultural practices. The embrace of automation and AI often centers on wealthy, tech-savvy regions, potentially leading to the oversight of underdeveloped areas and exacerbating global inequalities. Driven by advancements in robotics, artificial intelligence (AI), and digital technologies, automation is transforming societies and economies around the world [16]. Its impacts are varied, affecting economic systems, social relationships, cultural beliefs, and governance frameworks. This provides an in-depth analysis of the social and global impacts of automation, drawing on case studies, current trends, and predicted developments.

6.3.7 Wages and Inequality

Automation frequently results in increased income inequality. Highly proficient workers capable of advancing new technologies see rising salaries, whereas low-skilled laborers face stagnant or declining wages. Developed countries are experiencing a decline in middle-skill jobs, whereas there is an increase in both low-skill and high-skill jobs. This gap is not as apparent in developing countries, although initial signs are emerging in nations such as Mexico and Brazil. Automation increases efficiency and stimulates economic growth. By 2030, AI might add approximately $13 trillion to global economic production, leading to a 16% rise in overall GDP [17].

6.3.8 Social Consequences

Automation could exacerbate income inequality, as high-paid workers and large tech firms capture a disproportionate share of the advantages, whereas low-income workers face heightened risks of unemployment. As job opportunities decrease, communities reliant on industries susceptible to automation, such as manufacturing, may experience economic downturns and social turmoil. The uneven distribution of new job creation and job losses can worsen regional disparities. The rapid progress of automation highlights the deficiencies in existing social safety nets. Reductions in training and diminished public support systems have caused a gradual and challenging economic transition for many workers. Investing in education has become essential today, and reskilling is vital for helping employees transition to new roles.

6.4 PRIVACY AND DATA SECURITY

Automation, especially fueled by AI and digital technologies, greatly impacts privacy and data security by introducing new vulnerabilities while also offering improved tools to protect sensitive information. Privacy involves the correct handling of personal and sensitive information, including its collection, storage, processing, sharing, and deletion, enabling individuals to maintain authority over their data. Data security involves protecting data from unauthorized access, breaches, leaks, or misuse through both technical and organizational means. In automation, these concepts involve employing automated systems and AI for surveillance, categorizing, safeguarding, and administering data while complying with privacy laws and protecting against cyber risks. AI models can inherit biases from their training datasets, leading to inconsistent privacy enforcement or inequitable access restrictions. A lack of clarity about AI choices can reduce trust and complicate compliance efforts [18]. Dependence on automated systems without adequate human oversight can create a false sense of security and lead to compliance issues or the mishandling of complex privacy concerns.

Data protection and privacy in automation involve the use of AI and automated tools to protect confidential data, enforce privacy laws, and meet compliance standards efficiently and at scale. While automation offers powerful tools for enhancing security and privacy, it requires careful implementation, ongoing oversight, and the integration of human expertise to address challenges such as bias, vulnerabilities, and compliance concerns. When implemented properly, automation improves data security, reduces costs, and builds trust in an increasingly digital landscape [19].

6.4.1 Safeguarding Sensitive Employee Data

Safeguarding sensitive employee data involves ensuring that all personal, financial, health, and employment-related information remains protected, private, and exclusively available to authorized individuals in compliance with legal standards and best practices. Safeguarding sensitive employee information entails securing personal, confidential, and work-related data of employees from unauthorized access, abuse, exposure, alteration, or loss. This involves creating security measures, access limitations, and data protection guidelines to ensure that this information remains private, safe, and used only for legitimate organizational purposes. Safeguarding sensitive employee data in automation requires a thorough approach encompassing technical, administrative, and physical security measures. This involves setting up robust access controls, utilizing encryption, implementing data loss prevention strategies, performing routine security audits, educating employees, and adhering to data privacy regulations.

6.4.2 Challenges of AI-Driven Data Processing Under Privacy Regulations

AI systems frequently need extensive datasets that contain personal and sensitive information. Maintaining compliance with regulations such as the GDPR, CCPA, or India's DPDPA regarding data usage can be complicated. AI models developed using employee data without clear consent might breach legal requirements. Numerous AI algorithms, particularly deep learning models, function as "black boxes." Explaining how decisions are reached or justifying them during audits becomes challenging. GDPR requires the "right to explanation" for decisions made automatically. Data gathered for a specific reason should not be reused indiscriminately for other purposes. AI models can repurpose data (such as by employing performance data to forecast turnover) without explicit consent. Privacy regulations mandate the collection of only essential data. AI flourishes on the richness of data, which can be at odds with this principle. AI might still uncover patterns that can lead to the reidentification of people in supposedly anonymized datasets. This may unintentionally result in privacy breaches even when identifiers or names are excluded. AI using biased past data can produce biased outcomes (e.g., in recruitment or advancement). This approach contravenes fairness principles and antidiscrimination regulations and may indirectly infringe on privacy standards. Organizations frequently utilize AI tools from third parties. Ensuring that vendors adhere to privacy laws (e.g., via data processing agreements) is a legal obligation that changes more rapidly than regulations do. Ambiguity regarding what is lawful, ethical, or enforceable complicates compliance efforts.

Figure 6.2 depicts the difficult aspects of data volume that companies encounter in the age of big data. At the heart lies the fundamental problem of handling enormous volumes of data, encircled by significant obstacles: Data deluge, highlighting the inundation of information; storage, the requirement to securely and efficiently store large datasets; processing, guaranteeing prompt and efficient analysis; and data management, encompassing the tasks of handling, organizing, and preserving data integrity. Other challenges include data heterogeneity, handling data from various formats and sources; data privacy and security, safeguarding confidential information; bias and representativeness, maintaining fairness and precision in datasets; and data access, providing data to appropriate stakeholders. Collectively, these interrelated challenges emphasize the intricacy of managing extensive data in contemporary organizations.

6.4.3 Case Studies

TechCore, Inc., is a global IT solution company that employs over 10,000 individuals in 15 countries. The organization provides cloud-driven HR and payroll solutions to corporate clients, managing substantial amounts of employee information

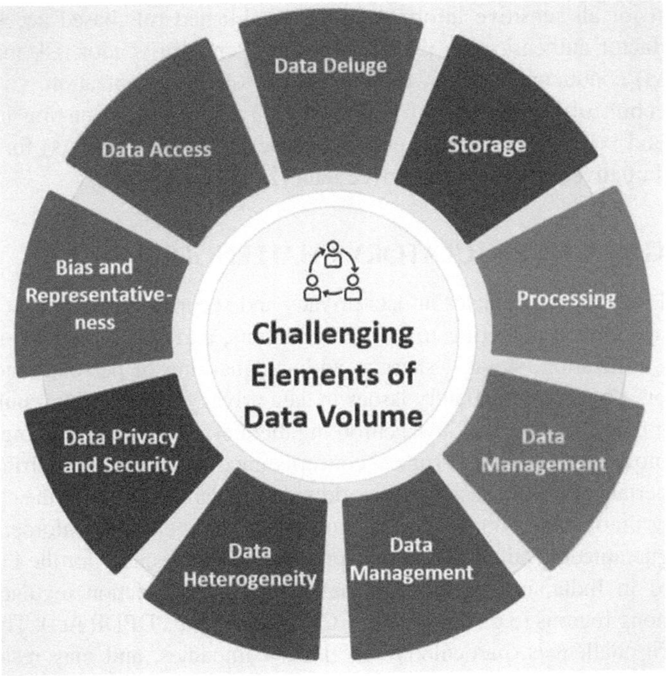

FIGURE 6.2 Challenging elements of data volume.

such as names, addresses, financial data, and health insurance details. In early 2023, TechCore experienced a significant data breach that revealed the personal information of more than 200,000 people, including workers from client firms. The breach was revealed when harmful individuals uploaded confidential employee information (salary details, health records, and ID numbers) onto the dark web [20]. The root causes were identified and are discussed here. Employee information was available to internal users outside of HR or compliance departments. Sensitive documents saved on internal servers lack encryption while at rest. The outdated payroll system contained unaddressed vulnerabilities. A third-party contractor employed for data analysis had inadequate security measures and served as the attack vector. Consent documentation was poorly organized, and a clear data retention policy was absent.

European regulators imposed a €3 million fine on the company for violations of the General Data Protection Regulation (GDPR) [21]. Contracts were terminated by clients, leading to a significant decline in employee trust. The violation resulted in more than $8 million in damage, attorney costs, and security enhancements. Data privacy and security should be preventive rather than responsive. Adhering to regulations is essential; laws such as the GDPR and DPDPA have significant repercussions. Vendors from outside the organization must adhere to the same security standards as the company. Openness and prompt reactions reduce certain harm, yet restoring trust is challenging. The measures that were implemented in this situation: i) informed regulators and impacted individuals within 72 hours, ii) engaged a cybersecurity firm to examine and address vulnerabilities, iii) applied end-to-end encryption for all sensitive information, iv) established role-based access controls and multifactor authentication (MFA), v) implemented a vendor risk management strategy, vi) conducted data privacy training across the organization, vii) created a data protection office (DPO), viii) adopted ISO 27001 for managing information security, and ix) required regular privacy impact assessments (PIAs) for any AI or analytics initiatives involving employee data [2, 22].

6.5 LEGAL AND REGULATORY CHALLENGES

Legal and regulatory obstacles in data privacy and security pertain to the challenges entities encounter in adhering to laws, regulations, and standards that oversee the collection, utilization, storage, sharing, and safeguarding of personal and sensitive information. Legal and regulatory issues in data privacy and security require traversing a complicated network of laws, enforcing them efficiently, and staying abreast of swift technological progress. Primary concerns encompass the extraterritorial application of certain laws, the absence of worldwide standardization, and the challenge of reconciling innovation with privacy safeguards. Creating efficient enforcement measures and guaranteeing adherence to data privacy laws, especially for the Data Protection Board in India, is a significant challenge. Data protection regulations differ greatly among regions (e.g., the GDPR, CCPA, and India's DPDP Act). This imposes compliance challenges, particularly for global companies, and may result in legal ambiguity and intricacy. Data localization demands, exemplified by India's DPDP Act, pose challenges regarding international operations and practicality. The swift advancement of technologies such as AI and big data analytics requires a careful equilibrium between promoting innovation and safeguarding personal privacy [23].

Organizations must openly share their data collection methods and take responsibility for their usage of personal information. Data breaches pose a significant threat, leading to financial and reputational repercussions. Companies require strong security measures and staff awareness to reduce these threats. Ethical considerations, such as reconciling personal preferences with compliance obligations, also influence data privacy and security. Companies are encountering personal data privacy issues in a rapidly changing digital era. Businesses that effectively address these challenges can secure a competitive edge in the market. The privacy of personal data is an essential element of a thorough data protection plan aimed at ensuring the secure collection, utilization, modification, retention, and sharing of information. It includes the ability of people to maintain their information confidentiality while promoting control over private data and safeguarding an individual's privacy. Personal data usually refer to information identified as personally identifiable information (PII), personal health information (PHI), or financial data, but they may also encompass details that are not exclusively personal [5]. In certain jurisdictions, sensitive information, known as special category data, demands enhanced protection. These data include personal details that indicate racial or ethnic background, political views, and religious or philosophical convictions; trade union affiliation; genetic information; biometric data used exclusively to identify an individual; health-related information; and data related to a person's sexual life or orientation. Publicly accessible personal data, whether deidentified or aggregated, are not subject to regulation.

The privacy of personal data is an essential aspect of a thorough data protection plan aimed at ensuring the secure collection, usage, modification, retention, and sharing of information. It includes the entitlement of people to maintain the privacy of their data while promoting the management of personal information and safeguarding an individual's secrecy. Personal data usually consist of information categorized as personally identifiable information (PII), personal health information (PHI), or financial details but may also encompass data that are not inherently personal [1]. In certain legal contexts, sensitive information, known as special category data, necessitates extra safeguarding. This information contains personal details disclosing racial or ethnic background, political views, and religious or philosophical beliefs; union membership; genetic data; biometric data used only for identifying an individual; health-related information; and data regarding a person's sexual life or orientation. Publicly accessible personal data, whether deidentified or combined, lack regulation. Legal and regulatory issues in privacy and data security focus on reconciling personal rights with the requirements of companies and governments, especially in the digital era. The principal challenges include the intricacies involved in managing various and changing regulations, the necessity of safeguarding personal information against breaches and exploitation, and the moral implications related to data gathering and utilization. The swift speed of technological progress, especially in AI and big data analytics, frequently surpasses the establishment of relevant regulations, resulting in new privacy issues. The vast amount of data gathered can complicate the tracking, management, and safeguarding of personal information efficiently.

6.5.1 Data Localization

The Act highlights data sovereignty by mandating that specific types of data be processed and stored in India [24]. This regulation raises concerns about whether companies can continue to operate globally and, more crucially, if it is practical to do so. Data localization denotes the legal or regulatory mandate that data, particularly personal or sensitive data, must be gathered, kept, and processed within the geographical limits of the nation where they are generated. The primary aim of data localization is to safeguard national security, maintain data privacy, and provide governments with enhanced control over citizens' information. It aids in enforcing local regulations, curbing data misuse by international actors, and fostering domestic digital infrastructure. Nonetheless, although it improves data sovereignty and security, it can also pose difficulties for international companies by increasing operational expenses and restricting the flow of data across borders.

6.5.2 Compliance and Awareness

SMEs focus primarily on compliance issues and awareness challenges. Certain individuals are not even conscious that they must adhere to the provisions of the DPDP Act of 2023, whereas others will be required to comply at a later time [25]. Moreover, adherence may prove difficult, requiring changes to infrastructure and the assignment of staff for training purposes. Compliance with data privacy signifies an organization's conformity with laws, regulations, and standards that dictate how personal and sensitive data must be collected, stored, processed, and shared. This guarantees that companies comply with regulations such as the GDPR, HIPAA, or local data protection laws to prevent legal liabilities, penalties, and damage to their reputation. Awareness in data privacy involves informing and raising consciousness among employees, stakeholders, and users regarding the importance of securing personal data, comprehending privacy rights, identifying threats such as data breaches, and adhering to best practices for protecting information. Compliance and awareness collectively constitute the cornerstone of a robust data privacy culture in organizations.

6.5.3 Balancing Innovation and Privacy

Big data is often crucial to India's flourishing IT industry, especially in AI and analytics. Facilitating and ensuring innovation while complying with privacy regulations is a difficult endeavor. Achieving a balance between innovation and privacy in data involves discovering the appropriate harmony between utilizing data for technological progress, customized services, and business expansion while simultaneously safeguarding individuals' privacy rights and guaranteeing the ethical handling of information [26]. Organizations frequently depend on large quantities of data for advancements in fields such as artificial intelligence, healthcare, and customer experience; however, misuse or reckless handling of personal data can result in trust erosion, regulatory infractions, and ethical issues. Thus, achieving balance necessitates the application of privacy-by-design principles, embracing transparent data protocols, and utilizing methods such as anonymization and encryption, allowing innovation to flourish without undermining the security, consent, and dignity of individuals.

6.5.4 Cross-border Data Transfers

As globalization increases, it becomes increasingly challenging to manage cross-border data transfers within the scope of the international frameworks one seeks to follow. Cross-border data transfer involves sending personal or sensitive data across international borders from one nation to another. This procedure is crucial for international commerce and digital interconnectivity, yet it is tightly controlled because of differing data privacy regulations across the globe, necessitating that organizations adhere to various legal structures to maintain data security and privacy.

6.5.5 Enforcement and Monitoring

The greatest challenge has been granting the Data Protection Board of India an independent and effective function. Considering the essential function the Board will have in establishing a robust Data Protection Authority, this specific challenge must be addressed for the Act to be executed properly. Enhancing capacity, engaging in public–private partnerships, and conducting necessary periodic assessments regarding legal frameworks in view of technological progress are various approaches to address such challenges [27].

6.5.6 AI Accountability: Who Is Responsible for Flawed Decisions?

Responsibility in AI is essential since it directly influences consumer trust, brand image, legal responsibilities, and ethical issues. AI-driven systems managing everything from customer engagement to strategic choices require accountability to be a primary consideration. A lack of clear accountability frameworks can result in operational risks, legal troubles, and harm to business reputation. The accountability terrain in AI is complex and involves various entities, each with distinct roles and obligations.

1. AI users: People managing AI systems bear the primary responsibility. Their duty involves comprehending the capabilities and possible constraints of the AI tools they utilize, guaranteeing proper usage, and maintaining diligent supervision
2. Supervisors need to confirm that their teams are properly educated to employ AI responsibly. They are responsible for overseeing AI applications in their teams, ensuring that they conform to the company's AI policy and guidelines
3. Companies/employers of AI users: Organizations utilizing AI in their processes need to set explicit protocols for its application. They are responsible for the outcomes of AI applications within their organization, necessitating strong risk management strategies and contingency plans for possible AI-related events
4. AI developers: AI responsibility applies to the people and groups that create AI systems, such as OpenAI. They are tasked with ensuring that the AI is developed and trained ethically, free from built-in biases, and with safeguards to avoid misuse or mistakes
5. AI vendors: Providers of AI products or services need to guarantee that they offer trustworthy, secure, and ethical AI solutions. They can be responsible if their product has issues or if they do not reveal possible risks and limitations to the client
6. Data providers: Since AI systems depend on data for their training and functioning, data suppliers are responsible for the quality and precision of the information they provide. They must also guarantee that the data are sourced ethically and comply with privacy regulations
7. Regulatory bodies: These organizations bear the primary responsibility for creating and implementing rules that regulate the application of AI. Their responsibility is to safeguard public and commercial interests, guarantee ethical AI implementation, and outline the legal framework that establishes accountability when issues arise.

This section discusses the intricacies of AI accountability. It is a complex matter that encompasses developers, deployers, and users of AI systems. AI systems, especially those employing machine learning, can develop decision-making methods over time, complicating the assignment of responsibility for particular choices [28]. Numerous AI systems function as "black boxes," with their internal mechanisms being unclear, even for those who have developed them. This absence of clarity hinders attempts to comprehend and correct mistakes. Various jurisdictions are crafting regulatory frameworks, such as the EU's AI Act, which establishes strict liability and fault-based liability for AI systems [29]. These rules seek to establish clear avenues for remedies while maintaining the necessity for innovation.

Entities employing AI must traverse a complicated legal framework. For example, the EU's suggested AI Liability Directive places proof responsibility on companies, making it necessary for them to show that their AI systems adhere to applicable regulations. This aims to ease the process by which victims pursue compensation for damage inflicted by AI. It is crucial to guarantee fairness, transparency, and accountability within AI systems. AI algorithm bias can reinforce current inequalities, whereas a lack of transparency may undermine trust. Ethical AI practices require thorough risk evaluations before implementation, informing users, and strong data governance structures. AI systems that learn from biased data may render unfair decisions, disproportionately impacting marginalized populations. This leads to ethical issues regarding the equity and justice of AI applications. AI accountability means that artificial intelligence should be created, implemented, and used in a way that allows responsibility for negative results to be attributed to responsible individuals. AI-driven technology frequently raises accountability issues because of the complexity and lack of clarity in machine and deep learning systems, the variety of stakeholders usually engaged in developing and deploying AI products, and the technology's ability to learn and adapt dynamically [30, 31].

AI systems frequently face criticism for being a "black box," indicating that the methodology behind generating an output cannot be entirely elucidated or understood by its users. If the decision-making of AI is not explainable or comprehensible, it becomes quite challenging to attribute responsibility and hold individuals accountable for damaging results.

6.5.7 Labor Laws and AI Compliance: Understanding Jurisdictional Nuances

Understanding the jurisdictional details of labor laws related to AI compliance is crucial for companies employing AI-based tools, as regulations vary significantly across different regions. Key issues include data privacy, algorithmic bias, and job impacts, with each region having a distinct regulatory framework. Regulations such as the EU's GDPR and India's Digital Personal Data Protection Act (DPDP) 2023 impact how AI systems handle personal data, require consent, minimize data, and restrict specific purposes. AI systems can amplify existing biases, leading to unfair or skewed outcomes. Officials find it challenging to address this issue, with some highlighting the need for transparency and accountability in AI decision-making procedures [9]. AI transforms the workplace, influencing job roles, work conditions, and the need for reskilling. Labor regulations must evolve in response to these developments, tackling concerns such as equitable pay, employment stability, and the influence of AI in managing the workforce. The Department of Labor has recently provided important guidance concerning the growing application of artificial intelligence in handling personnel, especially in HR procedures. This action is a direct reaction to the swift embrace of automated systems and emphasizes that employers must fully adhere to current labor standards, even while incorporating these technologies [32]. The guidance particularly emphasized vital aspects such as maintaining nondiscrimination in recruitment and performance assessments. Employers are directly reminded of their duty to assess AI systems to avoid generating or embedding biases that may violate employee rights. Moreover, DOL guidance emphasizes the existing obligation for employers to actively participate in sincere discussions with labor unions regarding the implementation of AI technologies, particularly related to monitoring in the workplace. This preliminary guidance provides a basic level of expectation, as organizations embrace AI, indicating that the journey to fully explore the intricate relationship between technology and worker protection while guaranteeing that AI does not diminish job quality or fairness is still in progress. This subtly warns that AI alone is not an easy path to compliance. By mid-2025, the legal framework regulating artificial intelligence usage in the workplace will still evolve quickly. Enhanced scrutiny is being introduced by different government tiers, indicating that this area is a significant priority. This year witnessed a considerable increase in states implementing their own targeted laws regarding AI in employment practices. For HR compliance managers, this entails remaining updated with an expanding array of regulations [16]. It emphasizes the essential requirement for employers to actively evaluate the AI tools they utilize, especially to detect and address possible biases, as well as to keep transparent records of how fairness and compliance are upheld. Although thorough federal AI regulations are still under discussion, it is evident that current labor and antidiscrimination laws are already relevant to automated decision-making processes that influence hiring, paying, or dismissal. The complexity brought by AI does not change the basic obligation; the employer still holds the responsibility for ensuring that AI systems adhere to all relevant labor standards. Steering through this changing landscape demands consistent focus, thorough assessment of technology, and readiness to adjust approaches to effectively handle shifting compliance risks.

6.5.8 The Future of Regulation for Generative AI in HR

Currently, businesses face a tight job market, elevated turnover rates, and employee stress, alongside the need to reskill, upskill, and strategically relocate personnel. Issues such as diversity and inclusion, organizational culture, and leadership development are crucial, and HR teams are concerned with employee experience, productivity, and internal effectiveness. The information in HR is scattered everywhere. A typical large corporation utilizes over 80 systems that interact with employees, and each system holds significant amounts of vital data to oversee its specific domain. When a business leader or executive aims to implement a change, assess a business situation, or improve a struggling team, they require all this information to be consolidated in a single integrated location. AI offers the opportunity to make this vision a reality (details below). While HR teams develop new initiatives and solutions, we are also facing a stressed workforce [33]. Workers are mostly overwhelmed (87% feel that they are at maximum capacity), so we need to streamline tasks, reduce the number of systems, and save time in administrative duties (allowing them to function at their highest capability). This signifies that HR teams are constantly confronted with the challenge of increasing service offerings while reducing their size and enhancing user-friendliness. AI assists with this. HR teams are ultimately evolving into creators, developers, and advisers. According to our systemic HR research, the future of HR involves fewer "support agents" and more "consultants, product managers, designers, and advisors." This indicates that an increasing number of HR teams are "creating things" and "examining things," which is fundamentally what generative AI performs. In a way, generative AI serves as an innovative answer to nearly every issue encountered by HR teams.

Currently, businesses are facing a competitive job market, elevated turnover rates, workforce stress, and the need to reskill, upskill, and strategically relocate employees. Issues such as diversity and inclusion, organizational culture, and leadership development continue to be crucial, whereas HR teams are concerned with employee experience, productivity, and internal effectiveness. HR data are scattered in various locations [34]. The typical large organization has over 80 systems with which employees interact, each containing extensive amounts of crucial data to assist in overseeing its specific domain. When a business leader or executive aims to implement a change, analyze a business situation, or address an underachieving team, they require all this information in a single consolidated location. AI holds the potential to make this vision a reality (details below). While HR teams develop new initiatives and solutions, we are also facing a stressed workforce. Workers are mostly exhausted (87% feel that they are functioning at maximum capacity), so we need to streamline tasks, cut down on systems, and free up time on administrative duties (allowing them to perform at their highest capability). This finding indicates that HR teams are consistently facing the challenge of increasing services while reducing their footprint and enhancing usability. AI assists with this [35].

HR teams are ultimately evolving into creators, developers, and advisers. According to our systemic HR research, the future of HR will feature fewer "support agents" and a greater presence of "consultants, product managers, designers, and advisors." This indicates that an increasing number of HR teams are "creating things" and "evaluating things," which fundamentally aligns with the primary function of generative AI. Thus, generative AI is the ideal fresh answer for nearly every issue that HR teams encounter. The second scenario involves enhancing overall productivity and subsequently reinvesting the time gained through the efficiency of GenAI. This situation develops a variant of the position—HR business talent strategists—to invest effort into enhanced employee engagement, change management, and more strategic talent planning.

In every case, both the HR organization and the overall executive leadership team will experience productivity improvements, but they need to choose between seeking immediate cost reductions or concentrating on enhancing talent effectiveness [36]. Regardless of the decision made by leaders, GenAI implementations might yield persuasive outcomes. Ultimately, HR leaders must possess a clear vision and a guiding principle for the function to direct such choices. GenAI goes beyond merely enhancing the efficiency of current processes and tasks. The technology enables HR to rethink its approach to supporting talent, thereby altering the entire HR delivery model. However, amidst such transformations, the human resources department must remain vigilant about the numerous risks associated with GenAI, particularly regarding the management of confidential employee data [37].

For years, HR has been striving to shape employee sentiment or reduce bias in immediate decision-making. When implemented effectively, AI can help further diminish the bias present in current processes. For accurate implementation, HR must collaborate closely with legal and business leaders to guarantee that responsible AI is utilized and that any biases present in GenAI systems are recognized and mitigated. Leaders need to expect a fluctuating technology and regulatory landscape in which new solutions and regulations are carefully observed. Humans continue to play a key role in these developments [38]. GenAI can recognize insights and condense information, but HR must guarantee that human beings make decisions that are logical, fair, and thoroughly recorded. This future relies on numerous factors, with HR's responsible application of GenAI being just one of them.

6.6 BEST PRACTICES FOR ETHICAL IMPLEMENTATION

The ethical implementation of generative AI (GenAI) is crucial for harnessing its benefits while minimizing risks such as bias, misinformation, privacy violations, and environmental impact. The key best practices distilled from current expert guidance and ethical frameworks are as follows. Disclose when and how generative AI tools are used, especially in academic, professional, or creative contexts. This builds trust and credibility by acknowledging AI's role in content creation. Whenever possible, provide information about the datasets used to train AI models and the limitations of the outputs. Transparency helps users understand potential biases and inaccuracies. Diverse and representative training data are used: bias in AI outputs often stems from skewed or incomplete training datasets. Data from various sources are incorporated to reduce systemic bias. Regularly audit AI outputs: Continuously monitor and evaluate AI-generated content for biased or offensive material and retrain models as needed to improve fairness. Augment, don't replace, human judgment: Use AI to support human decision-making rather than fully automating it, ensuring ethical oversight and contextual understanding. The input of sensitive, confidential, or proprietary information into AI tools that may store or reuse data should be avoided. Understand and comply with data privacy laws relevant to jurisdiction. Inform users about data use: Communicate how user data are collected, stored, and potentially shared by AI platforms to maintain informed consent [39]. Best practices for ethical implementation in generative AI refers to a comprehensive set of guidelines and principles designed to ensure that the development, deployment, and use of generative AI technologies (such as large language models, image generators, etc.) are conducted in a responsible, fair, transparent, and human-centric manner.

6.6.1 Development of Ethical Guidelines

AI ethics encompasses the standards and rules that regulate the responsible creation, implementation, and utilization of artificial intelligence (AI) technologies. It entails making certain that AI systems and applications conform to ethical norms, human values, and legal requirements. AI ethics aims to address potential risks and challenges linked to AI; encourage transparency, fairness, and accountability; and prevent any adverse outcomes stemming from AI decision-making. In the ever-evolving field of HR, the collaboration between artificial intelligence (AI) and human resources professionals is transforming the sector. Although AI cannot substitute the human element that characterizes HR's focus on people, its capacity for transformation is clear. By streamlining recruitment procedures and enhancing employee selection, as well as optimizing task assignments and utilizing predictive analytics for engagement, AI is transforming HR practices. A survey of 250 HR leaders, highlighted in Eightfold AI's report, "The Future of Work: Intelligent by Design," emphasized the extensive adoption of AI across different HR functions, such as employee record management, payroll processing, hiring, recruitment, performance evaluation, and onboarding [40]. The impact of AI on HR processes is extensive, enhancing a more streamlined and effective HR environment.

As HR leaders adopt AI technologies to improve employee experience, a comprehensive analysis of ethical aspects is essential. This investigation examines the careful and thoughtful incorporation of AI into HR practices, maintaining a harmonious relationship between innovation and ethical considerations. The fusion of artificial intelligence (AI) with human resources presents numerous opportunities and challenges. As HR leaders adopt AI to improve different functions, ethical issues become paramount. This section examines the moral consequences of AI in HR, investigating how companies can responsibly manage this changing environment while maintaining transparency, fairness, and ethical standards in their HR operations. To execute this evaluation successfully, organizations should form a cross-disciplinary team of stakeholders tasked with overseeing the ethics of AI. This cooperative team, potentially comprising members from HR, IT, legal, and other pertinent departments, is crucial in maintaining ethical standards, monitoring AI applications, and proactively tackling any ethical issues that could emerge. A strong evaluation of bias and fairness guarantees ethical AI usage and fosters transparency and equity in HR procedures.

I. **Avoid Invasion of Employee Privacy**: Privacy issues may emerge when AI tools that gather, retain, and examine personal information are employed. It is essential to ensure that candidates and employees are completely aware of how and why their data are managed, stored, and protected from unauthorized access. Emphasizing privacy and security is crucial in the implementation of AI in the workplace. While certain AI systems are intended to eliminate or avoid reusing user data, others may utilize information (such as voice commands, gender information, and language variations) to educate machine learning algorithms. This poses possible dangers to the privacy of workers or clients. Consequently, all information about employees, customers, or other sensitive facets of the organization should be anonymized before its use in AI applications [41].

II. **Ensuring Clarity and Fairness**: Transparency and clarity are vital ethical factors in the use of artificial intelligence within human resources. Business leaders need to emphasize transparency, especially when AI is utilized to oversee individuals or make choices that affect them directly. When an AI system makes decisions about employees, HR professionals must offer transparent explanations of the factors involved in that decision-making process. This dedication to openness boosts trust and responsibility in the application of AI in HR methods.

III. **Ensuring Human Control**: Maintaining human oversight is a key ethical principle in the use of artificial intelligence (AI) within human resources. Although AI can improve efficiency and decision-making, it is essential to maintain a balance with human supervision. Human oversight guarantees that AI systems adhere to ethical guidelines, fostering equity and avoiding unforeseen outcomes. HR professionals must maintain the power to intervene, interpret, and rectify the results produced by AI [42]. This human-centered approach protects against the excessive influence of AI, promoting a workplace where technology acts as a helpful resource under human oversight.

    Additionally, human oversight serves as protection against possible biases ingrained in AI algorithms. AI systems, by learning from past data, might unintentionally reinforce current biases. Human involvement is crucial for detecting, correcting, and addressing any discriminatory trends that may arise. HR experts, through their knowledge of organizational dynamics and varied workforce requirements, are essential in reducing bias and making sure that AI aligns with the organization's dedication to equity and inclusivity. By maintaining human oversight, organizations not only follow ethical AI principles but also promote a culture of accountability and transparency.

IV. **Build a Human-Centric AI System**: By focusing on a human-centered approach, organizations recognize the importance of maintaining the well-being, dignity, and rights of those affected. Creating AI systems that focus on the human experience guarantees equitable and impartial results, fostering inclusivity and reducing potential risks. A human-focused AI system prioritizes elements such as fairness, inclusivity, and safeguarding personal privacy. It aims to improve, not replace, human decision-making, encouraging cooperation between AI technology and human instincts. By engaging employees in both the development and execution stages, organizations can foster a system that reflects their values and ethical principles.

Essentially, a human-focused AI system aims to enhance human abilities, facilitate ethical choices, and maintain the values of fairness and respect in the HR field. It acts as a basis for establishing trust, promoting positive employee experiences, and addressing the ethical challenges linked to the incorporation of AI in HR practices. The rapid progress of artificial intelligence (AI) in human resources presents various opportunities, including enhancing talent acquisition, boosting employee engagement, and refining HR processes. Nonetheless, this swift development has also led to significant ethical issues in HR practices. The AI technologies employed in HR may unintentionally reinforce biases, affect employee rights, and create multiple ethical dilemmas. Following strict AI ethics and implementing strong data privacy protocols are crucial for avoiding ethical challenges in HR activities.

6.6.2 Privacy-First AI Design Principles

AI design principles that prioritize privacy focus on creating systems that center around user privacy, placing it as a priority from the earliest design phases through implementation and continued use. This entails integrating privacy safeguards into the system's design and capabilities instead of addressing them later as an additional concern. It involves being proactive, preventive, and user-focused, guaranteeing that privacy is the standard option and that users maintain control and clarity regarding their data. "Privacy-centered AI development" refers to a methodology for creating and implementing artificial intelligence systems, prioritizing the safeguarding of personal privacy as a core and essential tenet, which is embedded in every phase of the AI lifecycle from inception to execution and further. It is not an additional consideration or a supplement but rather a fundamental aspect of the system's design and functionality [43].

This idea is significantly shaped by the tenets of Privacy by Design (PbD), which was initially created by Dr. Ann Cavoukian, the former Information and Privacy Commissioner of Ontario, Canada. Rather than reacting to privacy breaches after they happen, privacy-first AI proactively identifies and mitigates privacy risks before they arise. This entails performing privacy impact assessments (PIAs) at the initial phases of AI development to recognize and address possible privacy risks. User privacy must be automatically safeguarded by default, without the need for individuals to perform specific actions to activate it. This indicates that AI systems are created to gather and handle only the essential personal data required and that data are safeguarded to the fullest extent automatically. Privacy is not an independent feature or a bonus addition; it is a fundamental aspect of the AI system's design and framework. Each choice, from gathering data to choosing algorithms and implementation, is made with privacy considerations. This principle dismisses the idea that privacy needs to sacrifice functionality or performance. Privacy-first AI seeks to ensure strong privacy safeguards while maintaining complete functionality, showcasing that privacy can foster innovation rather than impede it. Data utilized in AI systems must be safeguarded during their complete lifecycle, encompassing collection, processing, storage, and final deletion. This entails applying strict security protocols such as encryption (during storage, transfer, and utilization through methods such as homomorphic encryption) and powerful access restrictions.

This idea is strongly shaped by the tenets of PbD, initially formulated by Dr. Ann Cavoukian, the former Information and Privacy Commissioner of Ontario, Canada. Rather than waiting for privacy violations to occur and responding afterward, privacy-first AI predicts and mitigates privacy threats before they arise. This entails performing privacy impact assessments (PIAs) in the initial phases of AI development to recognize and address possible privacy risks [44]. User privacy should be safeguarded automatically by default, without individuals needing to take particular steps to activate it. AI systems are intended to gather and handle only the essential personal data needed, and that information is automatically safeguarded to the highest standard. Privacy is not an isolated feature or a supplementary addition; it is a fundamental part of the AI system's design and structure. Each choice, from gathering data to choosing and implementing algorithms, is made while considering privacy. This principle denies the idea that privacy should undermine functionality or performance. Privacy-centric AI seeks to provide strong privacy safeguards while maintaining complete functionality, showing that privacy can drive innovation rather than obstruct it. The data employed in AI systems must be safeguarded during their complete lifecycle, from gathering to processing, storage, and final deletion.

This includes applying stringent security protocols such as encryption (during storage, transmission, and even while being used via methods such as homomorphic encryption) and comprehensive access controls.

6.6.3 Building Transparent and Explainable AI Systems

Creating transparent and explainable AI systems in human resource management (HRM) is vital for promoting trust, guaranteeing fairness, adhering to regulations, and empowering HR professionals along with employees. AI in HR involves critical aspects such as recruitment, performance evaluation, and career advancement, where unclear choices can result in major adverse effects. Below is a thorough method for creating transparent and comprehensible AI systems in HR management:

I. **Foundational Principles**: The human effects of AI are always the top priority. Systems that enhance human abilities, promote equitable choices, and enable human supervision and intervention should be created. Ethical aspects (fairness, privacy, accountability) should be incorporated right from the start of the AI system's development process rather than as an afterthought. Guarantee compliance with applicable data privacy regulations (such as the GDPR, CCPA, and forthcoming AI-related laws such as the EU AI Act) and anti-bias legislation [45].

II. **Transparency Strategies**: Inform employees and candidates about when and how AI is utilized in HR procedures. Describe the function of the AI, the information it utilizes, and its possible effects. Refrain from using complex terms. Offer clear explanations of AI choices in straightforward, easy-to-understand terms for users without a technical background. Secure clear and informed consent from individuals regarding the gathering and utilization of their data by AI systems, particularly for sensitive personal information. For generative AI applied in HR (such as creating job descriptions or employee communications), the content generated by AI should be explicitly marked. The sources of all the data utilized to train the AI model are recorded. Be open about the methods of data collection and confirm that they are ethical and lawful. Gather and utilize only the essential data needed for the specific goal of AI. Frequently review training data for any biases (such as those linked to gender, race, or age) and proactively adopt measures to reduce them before they affect AI outcomes.

III. **Algorithm Transparency**: Maintain thorough documentation of the AI model's architecture; employ algorithms, parameters, and any identified constraints or presumptions. For AI in HR, specify which inputs (e.g., keywords from resumes, performance metrics) lead to certain outputs (e.g., invitations to interviews, recommendations for promotions). If feasible, offer a reason or explanation for the AI's choice. For example, if a candidate is selected, the system might highlight the key skills or experiences that influence the choice.

IV. **Explainability (XAI) Techniques**: Explainable AI (XAI) pertains to techniques that enhance the comprehensibility of predictions made by AI models for human users. In terms of human resources, this is essential for establishing trust and enabling appeals or interventions. Local interpretable model-agnostic explanations, or LIME, clarify the predictions of any classifier or regressor by locally approximating it with an interpretable model (such as a linear model) [46]. If an AI rejects an applicant, LIME might pinpoint which particular elements of their resume (e.g., absence of a certain skill, inadequate experience in an essential field) were most significant in the unfavorable outcome. This enables the applicant to grasp the reasons and possibly enhance for upcoming applications. SHAP provides each feature with an "importance" score for a specific prediction. It relies on game theory and equitably allocates credit (or blame) for a prediction across all features. During performance evaluations, if AI recommends a reduced rating, SHAP may indicate that the "project completion rate" and "team collaboration score" are the key negative contributors, whereas "attendance" has a smaller effect. This approach delivers explicit, practical insights to staff members. Numerous machine learning models (such as random forests or gradient boosting) can directly indicate the extent to which each input feature impacts the overall prediction throughout the dataset. In workforce planning, AI can foresee elevated turnover in a department.

Feature significance may indicate that "managerial backing" and "work-life harmony" are the key elements affecting retention in that division, directing HR initiatives. For easier classification tasks, decision trees generate a sequence of "if-then-else" rules that are naturally easy to understand. These rules clarify what changes in the input would prompt the AI to reach a different conclusion.

V. **Implementation Strategies for HRM**: Essential for important choices are choices with considerable consequences (hiring, promotions, disciplinary measures). AI is meant to serve as a recommender or aide, whereas a human HR professional ultimately makes the final decision. HR professionals must be able to examine AI suggestions, comprehend the reasoning behind them, and modify them if needed, ensuring a transparent audit trail for any modifications. The AI system's performance is typically assessed, with a focus on accuracy as well as fairness, bias, and consistency. Tools and methods are established to identify and assess bias in AI results over time, since model drift or data alterations may lead to new biases. Typically, whether AI explanations are genuinely clear and beneficial for HR professionals and staff is evaluated [47]. HR teams should be educated on the functionality of AI systems, how to analyze their results, and how to utilize explainability features efficiently. They are prepared to respond to employee inquiries regarding AI choices. Offer resources and accessible channels for employees to grasp the effects of AI on their roles and to request clarifications or contest choices. Defined pathways are created for HR professionals and employees to share their input on the AI system's effectiveness, equity, and transparency of its explanations. This feedback is used to progressively enhance the AI model and its features for explainability.

When third-party AI HR solutions are selected, vendors should be carefully assessed in terms of their dedication to transparency, clarity, bias reduction, and data confidentiality. Request comprehensive documentation and guarantees. Incorporate provisions in supplier agreements that outline transparency and explainability obligations [48]. By carefully implementing these principles and techniques, HR teams can progress beyond obscure "black box" AI systems to develop genuinely transparent and explainable AI that enhances efficiency while also promoting trust, fairness, and ethical decision-making in the organization.

6.7 CONCLUSIONS

Exploring the ethical and legal boundaries of new technologies, particularly artificial intelligence, necessitates a thoughtful and forward-looking approach. With AI systems becoming more embedded in society, they present substantial challenges concerning privacy, bias, and adherence to regulations. Concerns about privacy are prominent, as the gathering and handling of large quantities of personal information prompt inquiries regarding monitoring and personal rights. Bias and discrimination continue to pose ongoing threats, as AI systems might unintentionally reinforce or enhance current social inequalities if they are not thoughtfully crafted and overseen. Adhering to changing legal frameworks is also essential, necessitating that organizations remain updated on new regulations and establish strong governance strategies. Policymakers and stakeholders need to work together to create clear standards and accountability systems that ensure ethical design and supervision, protecting both personal and societal interests. In the end, the way forward involves enhancing transparency, encouraging equity, and incorporating ethical factors into each phase of technological advancement. In doing so, we can leverage the transformative power of AI and associated technologies while maintaining core values.

REFERENCES

1. Li, Z. (2024). Ethical frontiers in artificial intelligence: Navigating the complexities of bias, privacy, and accountability. *International Journal of Engineering and Management Research*, 14(3), 109–116.
2. Babikian, J. (2023). Navigating legal frontiers: Exploring emerging issues in cyber law. *Revista Espanola de Documentacion Cientifica*, 17(2), 95–109.
3. Chauhan, S., & Kumar, V. (2025). Virtual horizons: Navigating legal and ethical frontiers in HR virtual reality technology. In *The Future of HRM in a World of Persistent Virtual Reality* (pp. 167–195). Emerald Publishing Limited.
4. Rahimi, N., & Lee, S. (2025). Navigating the ethical landscape of big data collection and analysis. In *World Congress in Computer Science, Computer Engineering & Applied Computing* (pp. 99–108). Springer.
5. Gilbert, C., & Gilbert, M. A. (2024). The convergence of artificial intelligence and privacy: Navigating innovation with ethical considerations. *International Journal of Scientific Research and Modern Technology (IJSRMT)*, 3(9), 9–17.
6. Madhubala, R., Samad, S. R. A., & Thangam, S. (2024). Navigating ethical and privacy frontiers: Geospatial data in collaborative environments. In *Ethics, Machine Learning, and Python in Geospatial Analysis* (pp. 53–71). IGI Global Scientific Publishing.

7. Blessing, E. (2024). Regulatory compliance and ethical considerations: Compliance challenges and opportunities with the integration of Big Data and AI. https://doi.org/10.6084/m9.figshare.28528412
8. Mao, Q., & Xu, M. (2025). Navigating the ethical landscape of AI innovation: Challenges and opportunities. *International Journal of Digital Law and Governance*, 2(1), 197–221.
9. Kumar, A., & Kashyap, A. K. (2024). AI and business law: Navigating new frontiers. *California Management Review Insights*. https://cmr.berkeley.edu/2024/12/ai-and-business-law-navigating-new-frontiers/
10. Ashraf, M., & Haile, A. (2023). Data protection and AI: Navigating regulatory compliance in AI-driven systems. https://doi.org/10.13140/RG.2.2.13639.92328
11. Ajiga, D., Okeleke, P. A., Folorunsho, S. O., & Ezeigweneme, C. (2024). Navigating ethical considerations in software development and deployment in technological giants. *International Journal of Ethics and Research Utilization*, 7(1), 50–63.
12. Radanliev, P. (2025). Frontier AI regulation: What form should it take?. *Frontiers in Political Science*, 7, 1561776.
13. Kaduskar, V. P., Mhetre, H. V., Khatavkar, S. M., Chougule, P. A., Patil, M. V., Moje, R. J., & Naik, N. (2024). Navigating the frontier of generative AI integration in healthcare: Adoption, governance, and legal compliance. In *AI Healthcare Applications and Security, Ethical, and Legal Considerations* (pp. 261–289). IGI Global.
14. Sachdeva, C., Grover, V., Kaur, P., & Gangwar, V. P. (2024). Regulatory landscapes: Navigating compliance in the commercialization of basic science. In *Unleashing the Power of Basic Science in Business* (pp. 118–137). IGI Global.
15. Bahangulu, J. K., & Owusu-Berko, L. (2025). Algorithmic bias, data ethics, and governance: Ensuring fairness, transparency and compliance in AI-powered business analytics applications. *World Journal of Advanced Research and Reviews*, 25(2), 1746–1763.
16. Ali, A. (2024). Artificial intelligence and data privacy: Balancing innovation with security. *Frontiers in Artificial Intelligence Research*, 1(2), 289–328.
17. Corpuz, J. M. C. M., Cruzate, R. F., & Corpuz, J. T. (2025). Ethical considerations and challenges in maritime research: Addressing informed consent, privacy, and safety. In *Research Methods for Advancing the Maritime Industry* (pp. 281–312). IGI Global Scientific Publishing.
18. Yousuff, A., Abdullah, M., Ahmed, A. I., Abhishek, M., & Mishra, M. (2024). Navigating the landscape of large language models: Insights into AI algorithm bias, data security and advancements. *Srusti Management Review*, 1, 304–331.
19. More, M., Shah, S., Shelke, A., & Behare, N. (2025). Ethical and regulatory considerations in AI adoption within legal systems. In *Exploration of AI in Contemporary Legal Systems* (pp. 163–186). IGI Global Scientific Publishing.
20. Otieno, G., & Kiraka, R. (2024). Navigating the regulatory labyrinth: Compliance dilemmas and lead user innovation in the fintech sector. *Proceedings of the International Conference on Business Excellence*, 18(1), 2581–2593.
21. Jiao, J., Afroogh, S., Xu, Y., & Phillips, C. (2024). Navigating LLM ethics: Advancements, challenges, and future directions. *arXiv preprint arXiv*:2406.18841.
22. Ijaiya, H. (2024). Balancing data privacy and technology advancements: Navigating ethical challenges and shaping policy solutions. *International Journal of Research Publication and Reviews*, 5(12), 8118–8130.
23. Mohile, K. (2025). Navigating the balance: Ethics at the crossroads of healthcare data security and patient privacy. *World Journal of Advanced Research and Reviews*, 26(2), 4403–4412.
24. Ali, M. J. (2024). AI and the legal frontier: Balancing innovation and challenges in the age of artificial intelligence. *LawFoyer International Journal of Doctrinal Legal Research*, 2, 503.

25. Joseph, J. (2025). Ethical and legal frontiers in personalized genomics: Balancing innovation, privacy, and regulatory compliance. *International Journal of Innovation Studies*, 9(1), 1135–1151.
26. Dalippi, L., & Zuzaku, A. (2024). Navigating legal frontiers: Addressing challenges in regulating the digital economy. *Access to Justice in Eastern Europe*, 7(2), 1–26.
27. Majumder, S., & Dey, N. (2022). Explainable artificial intelligence (XAI) for knowledge management (KM). In *AI-empowered Knowledge Management* (pp. 101–104). Springer Singapore.
28. Alfonso, J. C. P., & Barrera, A. L. M. (2024). Into the metaverse: Navigating the ethical and legal frontier. *Nexus: Multidisciplinary Research Journal*, 1(2), 131–140.
29. Ghosh, S., Majumder, S., & Peng, S. L. (2023). An empirical study on adoption of artificial intelligence in human resource management. In *Artificial Intelligence Techniques in Human Resource Management* (pp. 29–85). Apple Academic Press.
30. Ahmad, N., Scholar, L. L. M., Haseeb, A., Iqbal, S., & Hassan, A. (2024). Navigating legal frontiers: Digital trade and data sovereignty in the contemporary legal landscape. *International Journal of Human and Society (IJHS)*, 4(1), 611–621.
31. Khanfir, M., & Karray, S. (2024). Navigating the AI frontier: Legal, ethical, and societal considerations for artificial personhood. *Journal of Ethics in Higher Education*, (4), 123–142.
32. Chen, W. (2024). Navigating the digital frontier: Challenges and opportunities in global media. *Global Media Journal*, 22(69), 1–3.
33. Dhirani, L. L., Mukhtiar, N., Chowdhry, B. S., & Newe, T. (2023). Ethical dilemmas and privacy issues in emerging technologies: A review. *Sensors*, 23(3), 1151.
34. Mujtaba, B. G., Vardarlıer, P., & Gündoğmuş, E. (2023). Digital diversity and inclusion: Agenda for data privacy and protection. In *Multidimensional and Strategic Outlook in Digital Business Transformation: Human Resource and Management Recommendations for Performance Improvement* (pp. 39–52). Springer International Publishing.
35. Sarmiento, C., Al-Qubaisi, M., Djibo, L. O., & Packham, J. (2024). Improving diversity and inclusion performance through the innovative application of technology and data. In *SPE International Conference and Exhibition on Health, Safety, Environment, and Sustainability*, Abu Dhabi, UAE, September 2024.
36. Chi, N., Lurie, E., & Mulligan, D. K. (2021). Reconfiguring diversity and inclusion for AI ethics. In *Proceedings of the 2021 AAAI/ACM Conference on AI, Ethics, and Society*, Virtual Event, USA, July 2021 (pp. 447–457).
37. van der Toorn, J., Veldhuizen, M. D., & Kulk, S. (2021). Researching the tension between privacy and inclusion in organizations: Promises and pitfalls of a transdisciplinary approach. *Tijdschrift voor Genderstudies*, 24(1), 53–63.
38. Liang, P. S., Kwon, S. C., Cho, I., Trinh-Shevrin, C., & Yi, S. (2023). Disaggregating racial and ethnic data: A step toward diversity, equity, and inclusion. *Clinical Gastroenterology and Hepatology*, 21(3), 567–571.
39. Shams, R. A., Zowghi, D., & Bano, M. (2025). AI and the quest for diversity and inclusion: A systematic literature review. *AI and Ethics*, 5(1), 411–438.
40. Zowghi, D., & Bano, M. (2024). AI for all: Diversity and Inclusion in AI. *AI and Ethics*, 4(4), 873–876.
41. Brown, J. A., Ward, A., & Duane, J. N. (2024). Data privacy, ethics and strategic leadership. In *Handbook of Research on Strategic Leadership in the Fourth Industrial Revolution* (pp. 330–347). Edward Elgar Publishing.
42. Kothapalli, S. (2021). Blockchain solutions for data privacy in HRM: Addressing security challenges. *Journal of Fareast International University*, 4(1), 17–25.

43. Wadhwa, S. N., Bhardwaj, G., & Srivastava, A. P. (2024). Analysis of techniques to ensure data security and employee privacy in E-HRM systems. In *2024 1st International Conference on Sustainable Computing and Integrated Communication in Changing Landscape of AI (ICSCAI)*, Greater Noida, India, July 2024 (pp. 1–6). IEEE.
44. Majumder, S., & Dey, N. (2022). *AI-empowered Knowledge Management*. Springer.
45. Jain, M. N., Maheshwari, M. M., Singhal, S., & Vishnoi, M. D. (2025). Cybersecurity in HR tech: A review of data privacy challenges in the digital HR ecosystem. *Advances in Consumer Research*, 2(2), 856.
46. Bhatti, M. A., & Alqasa, K. M. A. (2025). Digital integration in human resource management: Role of effective communication, data privacy and information accessibility. *Profesional de la información*, 34(1).
47. Kronivets, T., Yakovenko, O., Tymoshenko, Y., Ilnytskyi, M., Iasechko, S., & Iasechko, M. (2023). Legal and ethical dimensions of AI in education: Navigating new frontiers. *Review of Artificial Intelligence in Education*, 4, e21.
48. Yanamala, K. K. R. (2023). Transparency, privacy, and accountability in AI-enhanced HR processes. *Journal of Advanced Computing Systems*, 3(3), 10–18.

7 Future Trends and Strategic Insights

This chapter explores the dynamic development of generative artificial intelligence (GenAI; generative AI) and its impact on human resources (HR). As technology advances at breakneck speed, organizations need to predict and carefully assimilate new developments to maintain a competitive advantage, as they face challenges related to ethics, law, and operations. It also serves as a reference guide, describing key future directions in GenAI related to HR and providing pragmatic strategic advice. Its focus on the confluence of technology evolution with human-centered considerations means that innovations will be both new, equitable, and sustainable.

7.1 EMERGING TRENDS IN GENERATIVE AI FOR HR MANAGEMENT

Generative AI is transforming HR management by automating various processes, enhancing decision-making, and developing novel solutions for complex problems. As organizations increasingly embrace the use of AI-driven tools, there is a need to understand emerging trends effectively to tap into this potential. This section explores these trends, including increased productivity through ethical AI and innovations that are shaping the future of HR.

7.1.1 Increased Productivity with Ethical AI

Businesses today are increasingly using AI to be efficient and innovative. However, as the use of AI increases, it is important that these technologies are used in a fair manner. This subsection explores how the enhancement of AI and ethical approaches can be combined. It shows how organizations can use AI to increase productivity in a manner that does not compromise the principles of fairness, transparency, and accountability. Through the alignment of AI strategies with ethical concepts, organizations can make them more effective while simultaneously earning stakeholder trust and a positive impact on society.

7.1.1.1 Streamlining Recruitment Processes

Generative AI involves changing recruitment by automating tasks that usually take much time, making the process faster and more accurate. One of the greatest changes is in how resumes are screened. AI can quickly look at many resumes and compare candidates' skills and experiences to job requirements. This not only lowers the amount of work needed but also helps make candidate evaluation more consistent and fair, reducing the chances of human bias.

DOI: 10.1201/9781003674887-7

TABLE 7.1
AI Contributions to Recruitment Efficiency

Process	Traditional Method (Time Spent) (hours)	AI-Assisted Method (Time Spent) (hours)	Reduction (%)
Resume screening	20	4	80
Interview scheduling	10	2	80
Job description drafting	8	1	87.5

Another very important advantage of generative AI is its ability to write job descriptions. Using NLG, AI tools create clear, interesting, and tailored job descriptions that suit what a company needs and what is happening in the job market. This is helpful for saving time on HR professionals' behalf while keeping up high standards, making the hiring process smooth and efficient.

Moreover, generative AI has advanced candidate experience through personalized communication. AI-powered chatbots and virtual assistants interact with candidates instantly, where queries are answered, updates are given, and the overall application process is guided. This level of personalization improves candidate experience, fosters engagement, and helps build a positive employer brand for the organization.

Table 7.1 shows the measurable impact of generative AI on key recruitment processes and time efficiency by comparing traditional methods with AI-assisted approaches. The table presents three critical recruitment tasks, that is, resume screening, interview scheduling, and job description drafting, and quantifies the time savings with AI integration.

7.1.1.2 Enhancing Employee Experience

Generative AI has been able to considerably enhance the employee experience by using AI-powered chatbots and virtual assistants that are available to support employees at all times. These tools provide instant answers to most employee queries, such as clarifications on HR policies, payroll issues, and benefits information, thus reducing dependence on HR personnel. These systems allow HR professionals to focus on more strategic tasks rather than repetitive routine inquiries, hence enhancing overall workplace productivity. This also allows for a better and more responsive work environment since AI integration in employee support systems encourages the feeling of being valued and supported when issues are dealt with immediately, which improves job satisfaction and engagement. In this regard, however, ethical considerations play a critical role in designing and implementing such tools. Transparency in the collection and processing of such data, along with adherence to set data privacy regulations, leads to trust and safety in these AI systems. According to research conducted by [1], fairness and inclusivity are critical components of these tools to become not only operationally efficient but also equitable and inclusive in their dealings with employees.

Such positive effects of AI, for example, are now manifested in the steady increase in satisfaction rates over the past few years. As indicated in Figure 7.1,

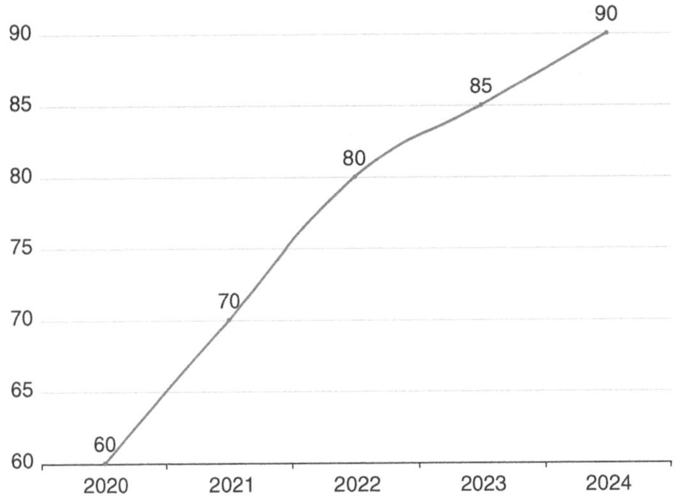

FIGURE 7.1 Employee satisfaction with AI assistance (2020–2024).

the data reflect how organizations that have begun to adopt AI for employee support have seen a consistent increase over the years from 2020 to 2024 in terms of satisfaction metrics, thereby being able to participate in creating a more supportive and engaging work environment through AI.

7.1.1.3 Bias Mitigation in Decision-making

The generation of AI may provide insights and uncover hidden biases in HR processes by promoting fairness and diversity in an organization. For large datasets, AI models identify patterns and inconsistencies that might lead to biased results. They then alert the HR professional about such instances for correction. This means applying adversarial debiasing—that is, training the AI system to minimize bias with controlled processes involving adversarial feedback—and applying the models via ethical frameworks to achieve fair outputs. The use of such techniques reduces risks for discriminatory practices that might incidentally come with historical data and unequal distribution in decision-making. One of the most significant examples of such effectiveness is demonstrated by [2], who, after the implementation of bias-detection algorithms, showed a 15% improvement in diversity metrics within recruitment processes. This improvement demonstrates how strategically applying bias-mitigation techniques can lead to more inclusive and representative hiring practices, further promoting a fairer and more diverse workforce.

7.1.2 Innovations and Future Directions

The integration of cutting-edge technologies, particularly generative AI, is driving transformative changes in the landscape of HR management. Innovations in AI not only enhance existing HR practices but also pave the way for new approaches to talent acquisition, employee engagement, and organizational development. In the following section, we explore the still-emerging trends in AI-driven HR systems: advancements in automation, personalization, and predictive analytics. We will also consider possible future directions, keeping in mind that these technologies should enable more inclusive, data-driven, and adaptable HR environments. In this context, fast-paced AI innovation promises to change HR processes in ways that were previously unimaginable and better support efficiency, deeper insights, and more personalized experiences for both the employee and employer. As we look forward to the future of AI in HR management, we have new ethical considerations associated with such advancements.

7.1.2.1 Personalized Learning and Development

AI-driven platforms are increasingly being used to analyze employee performance and provide personalized recommendations for training and development. Using advanced technologies such as natural language processing (NLP) and adaptive learning models, these platforms can offer real-time feedback that aligns with an employee's current performance, learning style, and development needs. NLP enables the system to interpret and respond to interactions with employees. Adaptive learning models adapt the training content on the basis of an individual's progression, which guarantees continuous and effective skill development. These systems not only improve learning but also help employees develop their potential by offering the right resources at the right time and in the right context. Nusair [3] reported that organizations that implemented AI-powered training platforms experienced a 25% increase in employee productivity. This improvement can be attributed to the personalized, efficient training these systems provide, ensuring that employees receive the right training at the right time, thus improving both their individual performance and overall organizational outcomes.

As shown in Table 7.2, key statistics of employees before and after AI show that one of the important variables is improvement in training completion. With an average score of 65% at AI implementation to an average of 85%, an improvement rate of 30%, it is an indication of a positive response toward employee engagement that helps trainees stay interested in completing training. The knowledge retention rate, which represents the amount of information employees can retain 6 months after training, also improved by 40%, moving from 50% before AI to 70% after AI. This result suggests that AI-based training systems are more efficient at ensuring that

TABLE 7.2
Impact of AI on Employee Training Outcomes

Metric	Pre-AI Implementation (%)	Post-AI Implementation (%)	Improvement (%)
Training completion rate	65	85	30
Knowledge retention (6 months)	50	70	40
Employee engagement	60	80	33

employees retain key skills and knowledge over time. This could be because AI training systems provide continuous feedback that can help employees learn better through adaptive content. Finally, employee engagement in training also increased significantly, from 60% before the implementation of AI to 80% afterward, an increase of 33%. All these improvements are because AI can tailor a training experience for each individual, provide real-time feedback, and even adjust content to make it relevant and interesting. Overall, the data indicate that AI adoption in training programs significantly improves training completion, knowledge retention, and employee engagement, thus leading to more effective and impactful training outcomes.

7.1.2.2 AI-Driven Workforce Analytics

AI-driven workforce analytics are transforming the way an organization understands and manages its HR. Generative AI will power advanced analytics that can provide insights into numerous workforce dynamics, such as attrition trends, employee engagement, and productivity metrics. Organizations can make decisions on the basis of those insights and handle issues before they become major issues. For example, predictive analytics can identify early signs of employee turnover by analyzing patterns in job satisfaction, work behaviors, and external factors, allowing HR teams to take proactive steps to retain top talent. Similarly, AI can evaluate employee engagement levels, helping organizations tailor their strategies to increase morale and productivity. Beyond just knowing the current situation, these tools allow for the prediction of future trends, which enables organizations to better plan for future workforce needs. However, the integration of AI in workforce analytics must be accompanied by ethical considerations, ensuring that data are used responsibly, with respect to privacy, and without reinforcing biases. By balancing advanced data analysis with ethical decision-making, AI-driven workforce analytics can empower HR departments to make proactive, equitable, and informed decisions, thus improving both organizational efficiency and employee satisfaction.

7.1.2.3 The Role of Explainable AI (XAI)

With increasingly complex HR systems, the demand for transparency and accountability in AI-driven decision-making processes has grown to unprecedented levels. Explainable AI (XAI) plays a critical role in this regard. XAI can be defined as techniques and methods aimed at making decisions by AI systems understandable to humans, offering clear explanations about how and why a particular outcome is generated. In HR systems, where hiring, promotion, and employee performance evaluation decisions have deep repercussions, the need to explain AI-driven decisions will help build trust with employees and other stakeholders. If transparency is lacking, employees may become alienated or distrustful of the decisions of AI systems, which negatively affects morale, engagement, and overall organizational culture.

Moreover, explainability is critical to compliance with ethical standards and legal regulations, such as data protection laws such as the General Data Protection Regulation (GDPR). In most jurisdictions, organizations are mandated to explain automated decisions that significantly affect individuals, and a failure to provide such explanations may have legal consequences. XAI techniques enable HR professionals

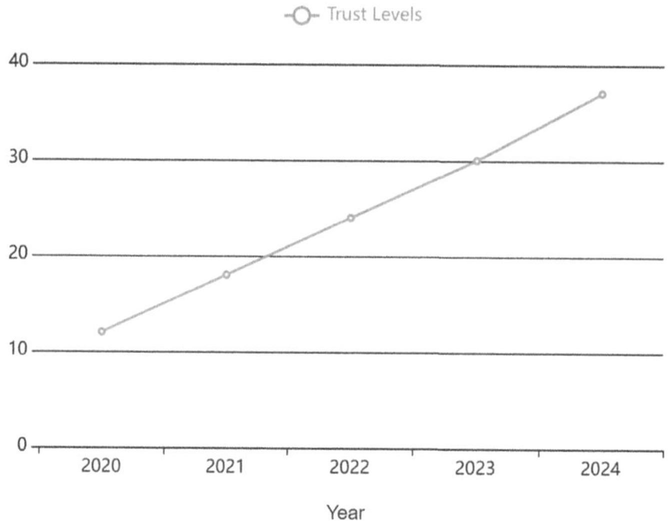

FIGURE 7.2 Trust levels in AI-driven HR systems (2020–2024).

to understand how an AI model comes to a decision so that one can verify whether those decisions are fair, consistent, and bias-free. Therefore, through this type of XAI, there will be an increased level of trust in the use of AI technologies, while at the same time, it will ensure that such systems operate within organizational values and ethical standards to provide an equitable and just workplace. Research by Ezeji et al. [4] revealed that implementing XAI improved stakeholder confidence by 40%.

Figure 7.2 represents the trends in trust levels of AI-driven HR systems before and after the introduction of XAI from 2020 to 2024. The graph shows a comparison of trust levels when AI systems were used in HR without any transparency mechanisms, which was the case before the introduction of XAI, and trust levels after the introduction of XAI, where the decision-making process of the AI system is explainable and understandable by the user.

7.2 GLOBAL PERSPECTIVES ON AI IN HR

AI is transforming HR management around the globe, thereby giving organizations an easier way to organize processes, improving decision-making quality, and enhancing engagement between employees. The adoption of AI in various geographic regions differs widely depending on local cultural, economic, and legal factors. This chapter discusses international views on AI in HR and how AI has been adopted in different geographic areas, along with the critical awareness needed for cross-cultural adaptation.

7.2.1 Adopting AI Across Diverse Geographic Regions

The adoption of AI in HR is not universally uniform. Developed economies, such as the United States, the United Kingdom, and Japan, are primary users of AI in HR.

These regions benefit from robust technological infrastructures, significant investments in AI research, and a workforce accustomed to digital transformation. According to Deloitte's (2021) study [5], 75% of companies in North America have applied AI to at least one HR function. This can be attributed to advanced technology ecosystems, a culture of innovation, and the availability of skilled professionals well versed in AI-driven tools.

While economies from Africa, Southeast Asia, and Latin America have their own set of problems regarding adopting AI in HR, they face unique challenges. Access to cutting-edge technology remains limited, whereas digital literacy levels are lower among the workforce. Additionally, financial resources are inadequate. For example, many organizations in those areas lack the infrastructure needed to effectively deploy AI-powered solutions. Despite these challenges, emerging markets offer unique opportunities for innovation. Mobile-based AI solutions have found great traction in Africa, which uses high mobile penetration rates to overcome the traditional infrastructure barrier. These solutions are particularly useful in recruitment and employee engagement, as they enable organizations to connect with talent pools that may otherwise be inaccessible [6].

Moreover, localized approaches to AI adoption show how technology can be adapted to meet regional needs. For example, in Southeast Asia, AI tools that can handle multilingual environments are crucial because of the linguistic diversity of the region. Similarly, Latin America has seen an increasing application of AI in sectors such as retail and manufacturing, where workforce management tools are optimized for local market conditions. However, these applications face problems such as inconsistencies in data quality and a shortage of skills. Therefore, targeted investment in both technology and human capital development is needed.

7.2.1.1 Case Study: AI in Recruitment in India

India is a very good example of how AI can be adapted to the specific needs of a place. Indian companies use AI-powered platforms to screen large volumes of job applications efficiently because of the vast and diverse labor market in the country. Tools such as HireVue and Belong.ai have been customized to account for linguistic diversity and local hiring practices [7]. This localized approach ensures that AI solutions are not only efficient but also culturally relevant.

7.2.1.2 Regional Challenges and Opportunities

1. **North America and Europe**: These regions have emerged as global leaders in the development of ethical AI and regulatory compliance. Strict data privacy laws, such as the GDPR in Europe, have created a framework that ensures transparency, accountability, and fairness in AI applications. Companies in these regions spend significantly more on ethical AI initiatives by incorporating responsible practices into HR functions such as recruitment, performance management, and employee engagement. The presence of full-fledged ecosystems of mature AI and a workforce skilled and knowledgeable in these digital technologies augments these successes. Moreover, governments, private sectors, and academic institutions facilitate innovation with the utmost adherence to moral standards [8].

2. **Asia-Pacific Region**: The Asia-Pacific region is experiencing tremendous adoption of AI in HR through large-scale digital transformation projects and increased demand for technology solutions in fast-growing economies. Some of the most significant leaders in AI-driven HR innovations are China, India, and Singapore. However, linguistic diversity and cultural nuances stand as major hurdles. AI systems must manage multiple dialects and accommodate diverse communication styles across the region. For example, hierarchical work cultures in Asian countries demand AI systems that honor traditional values while allowing contemporary HR practices to be implemented. Thus, there is increasing intergovernmental and corporate coordination in the development of AI plans in the region. Notably, this study focuses on how recruitment and talent management applications under AI are contextualized to accommodate regional languages and cultural practices, thereby offering greater uptake.
3. **Latin America**: AI adoption in Latin America is steadily increasing in retail, manufacturing, and financial services. However, this is not the same case for many AI-driven HR solutions that require implementation on a large scale. Skill shortages, poor-quality data, and a lack of advanced infrastructure are still the main barriers to overcome. In fact, solutions to overcome such gaps are underway. For example, training programs for AI and partnerships with international tech firms are helping develop the skills of the local workforce. Furthermore, customized AI applications such as chatbots for customer service and predictive analytics for workforce planning are being used to suit the economic and cultural context of the region. Organizations in Latin America are also working on cost-effective solutions by using open-source AI tools to address resource constraints (Table 7.3).

7.2.2 Cross-Cultural Adaptation Awareness

Cross-cultural adaptation is a critical factor in the successful implementation of AI in HR. AI systems are often global in nature and operate across diverse cultural landscapes where values, communication styles, and workplace norms can vary

TABLE 7.3
Regional Challenges and Opportunities

Region	Opportunities	Challenges
North America and Europe	Ethical AI development, strong regulatory frameworks, skilled workforce	High implementation costs, regulatory complexity
Asia-Pacific	Rapid digital transformation, tailored multilingual solutions	Linguistic diversity, cultural nuances, hierarchical workplace norms
Latin America	Growth in retail and manufacturing, cost-effective solutions	Skills shortages, poor data quality, limited infrastructure

significantly. Without adequate cross-cultural adaptation, AI tools risk perpetuating biases, misinterpreting user inputs, or failing to meet the needs of a diverse workforce. For example, an AI system designed for Western workplace cultures may focus on individual achievements and may miss collective-oriented practices, which are more common in many Asian or African contexts.

AI systems must be designed to respect and include cultural nuances by enhancing their strength to facilitate inclusivity. That is, the training of AI on relevant datasets that portray diverse cultural contexts and experiences should minimize bias and ensure fair treatment of all users. There is also a need to engage local experts in design to understand local behaviors in the workplace, such as preferred communication styles, decision-making hierarchies, and culturally significant practices such as observance of holidays or customary greetings.

Cross-cultural adaptation also requires an active effort in identifying and eliminating any potential cultural bias embedded in AI algorithms. For example, language processing models have to factor in variations in tone, politeness, and idiomatic expressions between languages. Similarly, recruitment AI tools must be fine-tuned to recognize how skills and experience are represented by different candidates from various cultures and avoid biasing in favor of some characteristics and not others.

For cross-cultural adaptation to succeed, continuous learning and feedback in organizations is paramount. User feedback loops within AI systems facilitate evolution and improvement in tandem with regional expectations. The performance of AI systems may be reviewed on a periodic basis in various cultural settings, leading to areas for improvement, such as the algorithms of AI to account for regional gender dynamics or changing the user interface in accordance with the preferences of a region.

The embedding of cultural intelligence into AI systems can help organizations reap several benefits, such as increased user satisfaction, broader adoption of AI tools, and enhanced equity in HR practices. Ultimately, cross-cultural adaptation is not just a technical challenge but also a vital ethical imperative that aligns AI applications with the values and needs of a global workforce.

7.2.2.1 Addressing Cultural Bias in AI

One of the greatest concerns on the global scale of AI is its cultural bias. AI systems learn from datasets overwhelmingly sourced from a single geographic region and perpetuate biases through application in the rest of the world. For example, an AI system may be biased toward skewed decision processes, misinterpreting user input, and not considering culturally specific practices. For example, an AI algorithm trained on Western-centric data may emphasize direct communication styles and individual achievements, potentially overlooking the importance of hierarchical respect, collective decision-making, and indirect communication, which are prevalent in many Asian cultures [9]. This misalignment can result in AI systems delivering suboptimal or even counterproductive outcomes in non-Western contexts.

Addressing the issue of cultural bias requires multilateral approaches in the training phase of AI. The first concern is that diversified datasets should incorporate richness in global cultures, languages, and ways of working. These diversified datasets should include inputs from other underrepresented areas to ensure representative balance and be less likely to harbor stereotypes. For example, the inclusion of linguistic nuances and formal honorifics used in some cultural contexts can greatly enhance cultural sensitivity in any natural language processing application.

Cultural intelligence must be incorporated into AI system design, with consideration of regional norms, values, and practices. This could involve collaboration with local experts in the development phase to identify cultural elements that AI needs to respect and integrate. For example, recruitment algorithms can be adjusted to recognize culturally specific qualifications or work experiences so that candidates from diverse backgrounds are judged fairly. Continuity in monitoring and fine-tuning AI systems is, therefore, also crucial to address arising biases. There should be some kind of feedback loop, user reviews, and periodic auditing processes that help reveal cultural insensitivities or inaccuracies while functioning. Iterative improvement practices enable organizations to continue their AI system in alignment with the changing dynamics of the desired regions.

Finally, global collaboration among policymakers, technologists, and cultural scholars will be necessary to develop standards and best practices for culturally adaptive AI. Initiatives such as these can foster the development of ethical frameworks that prioritize inclusivity and fairness, creating a benchmark for AI deployment in diverse cultural environments. Ultimately, cultural bias in AI is not just a technical challenge but also a necessary step toward creating equitable and globally relevant AI solutions.

7.2.2.2 Building Inclusive AI Systems

Building inclusive AI systems is the cornerstone of effective cross-cultural adaptation, ensuring that AI technologies are accessible, fair, and responsive to the diverse needs of global users [10]. Inclusivity is essential for mitigating biases and fostering equitable outcomes in HR practices. This is achieved through a variety of strategies, such as localized language support, cultural sensitivity training, and user feedback integration.

- **Localized Language Support**: Developing AI systems that are multilingual and can handle various dialects will be one of the prime means to incorporate a sense of inclusivity. That would essentially involve building models for NLP to accurately interpret regional languages, colloquialisms, and expressions within context. An AI-based customer service or recruitment tool would require this to accommodate linguistic diversity that can be witnessed in countries such as India, with over 20 official languages. Localized language support not only increases the user experience but also ensures that AI systems can effectively communicate with and cater to diverse populations.
- **Cultural Sensitivity Training for AI Models**: Cultural sensitivity must be an essential part of truly inclusive AI. AI tools must be programmed to recognize cultural norms, be they holiday calendars, gender roles, or workplace hierarchies. The AI scheduling tool used in the Middle East must

account for times of prayer and religious holidays; the recruitment platform in Japan respects hierarchical job titles and formal communication protocols. Cultural sensitivity training involves analyzing region-specific data and embedding cultural intelligence into the system's algorithms so that AI systems are aligned with local values and practices, thereby minimizing the risk of cultural insensitivity or misalignment.

- **User Feedback Loops**: Continuous user feedback is important for perfecting AI systems and addressing any inadvertent cultural insensitivity. This helps developers identify improvement areas and adjust the system according to the input of diverse user groups. For example, employees in Latin America may comment that an AI tool designed for performance evaluations needs to take into account regional preferences for collaborative achievements over individual accomplishments. Updating in real time according to user insight ensures that the AI system remains relevant, effective, and inclusive over time.

7.2.2.3 Global Examples of Cross-cultural AI Implementation

- **China**: China has been at the forefront in terms of how AI can be connected to local business practices and social norms. AI-based tools such as WeChat Work are designed to highlight efficiency and collective decision-making, which are major cultural priorities of the country, with a focus on group harmony and productivity. These tools are designed for multilingual interactions and help carry out communications across diverse teams without issues, which has been highly effective in workplaces across China.
- **Middle East**: The style of AI applications in HR departments in the Middle East is designed with sensitive reverence to religious observances. For example, the intelligent systems used in workforce scheduling consider daily prayers as well as prayers during Ramadan. In this manner, culturally aware features, such as the consideration of local values, ensure that AI tools operate accordingly, thereby building trust and acceptance among their users.
- **Scandinavia**: The approach of Scandinavia to AI implementation reflects its cultural orientation toward employee well-being and work–life balance. The AI-based scheduling and performance management systems prioritize a fair distribution of workload, flexible working hours, and openness in the evaluation process. Scandinavian organizations serve as role models by developing AI for humane and ethical HR practices, which is a benchmark for other regions.

The adoption and adaptation of AI in HR are deeply affected by geographical and cultural contexts. Developed economies are leaders in technological advancements, whereas emerging economies are at the forefront of innovative localized applications of AI. Therefore, cross-cultural adaptation and inclusivity are very important for the global success of AI in HR. Future research could focus on developing frameworks for culturally adaptive AI systems and studying their long-term effects on workforce diversity and inclusion.

REFERENCES

1. Oyekunle, D., Boohene, D., & Preston, D. (2024). Ethical considerations in AI-powered work environments: A literature review and theoretical framework for ensuring human dignity and fairness. *International Journal of Scientific Research and Management (IJSRM)*, 12(3), 6166–6178. https://doi.org/10.18535/ijsrm/v12i03.em18
2. Bar-Gil, O., Ron, T., & Czerniak, O. (2024). AI for the people? Embedding AI ethics in HR and people analytics projects. *Technology in Society*, 77, 102527. https://doi.org/10.1016/j.techsoc.2024.102527
3. Nusair, R. (2024). The impact of artificial intelligence on human resource practices and employee experience. https://www.researchgate.net/publication/384397723_The_Impact_of_Artificial_Intelligence_on_Human_Resource_Practices_and_Employee_Experience
4. Ezeji, N. G., Chibuezeand, K. I., & Nwobodo-Nzeribe, N. H. (2024). Enhancing trust and transparency in AI: A comprehensive study on explainable artificial intelligence (XAI) techniques and applications. *Presented at the 2024 International Conference of Engineering Innovation for Sustainable Development (ICEISD)*, Enugu, Nigeria, July 2024. https://doi.org/10.5281/zenodo.13889644
5. Deloitte. (2021). Global human capital trends: Special report on AI adoption in HR. https://www.deloitte.com/uk/en/services/consulting/research/global-human-capital-trends-2021.html
6. UNCTAD. (2023). Digital economy report: AI in emerging markets. https://unctad.org/tir2023#:~:text=The%2017%20frontier%20technologies%20covered,leaving%20developing%20economies%20further%20behind
7. Mehrotra, S., & Khanna, A. (2022). Recruitment through AI in selected Indian companies. *Metamorphosis*, 21(1), 31–39. https://doi.org/10.1177/09726225211066220
8. European Commission. (2020). General Data Protection Regulation (GDPR): Implications for AI in HR. https://www.europarl.europa.eu/RegData/etudes/STUD/2020/641530/EPRS_STU(2020)641530_EN.pdf
9. Hofstede, G., Hofstede, G. J., & Minkov, M. (2010). *Cultures and Organizations: Software of the Mind*, Third Edition. McGraw Hill LLC.
10. Majumder, S., & Dey, N. (2022). *AI-empowered Knowledge Management.* Springer.

8 Conclusion

Generative AI is now not a future trend but rather a here-and-now force that transforms the way organizations manage human resources (HR). The book has followed the development of the role of AI in HR, from an initial conceptual basis through real-world applications, ethical considerations, and strategic thinking for the future. Taken together, the book illustrates that the integration of generative AI is more than a technological enhancement—it is a paradigm shift in how HR professionals recruit, develop, engage, and retain talent.

Chapter 1 presents the foundations of generative AI and positions it against conventional HR systems. This study highlights the potential along with the problems associated with integrating AI into HR functions, demonstrating how businesses, including Small and Medium Enterprises (SMEs), can achieve cost and operational savings through smart adoption. Chapter 2 emphasized the ways in which recruiting processes are revolutionized by generative technologies, starting from generating maximally effective job ads to automatically resume screening and improving candidate experience. The chapter showed how these tools power efficiency, eliminate bias, and customize engagement with job candidates.

Chapter 3 progressed from recruiting to employee retention and discussed how AI can be applied in the onboarding and training of employees. Organizations can use automated onboarding programs and adaptive learning platforms to set employees up for longevity. The case studies highlight the value of predictive analytics, which can help organizations identify gaps in skills and offer tailored development opportunities. Chapter 4 transitions to consider the engagement and retention of employees and explains how personalized, AI-powered strategies help organizations of any size build customized career development pathways, enhance recognition programs, and engage in data-based decisions around succession planning for leadership. All these changes improve culture and engagement over time.

Chapter 5 approaches the operational aspect of AI adoption and introduces a framework to assist organizations with readiness for AI adoption, including myth-busting, evaluating their organizational needs for AI, finding a vendor, and ensuring data and compliance. Most importantly, it also outlines the human aspect of the transformational journey and emphasizes that it might be just as important to inspire HR teams to embrace these changes and to build an organization to sustain continuous learning. Finally, Chapter 6 discusses the ethical, legal, and privacy issues associated with HR-driven AI. This confirms the need to consider biases, accountability, and regulatory implications of AI implementation while also highlighting the need for transparency, fairness, and human explainability of the systems. The best practices for ethical AI adoption are presented to guide practitioners in maximizing their use of AI systems responsibly.

Finally, Chapter 7 concludes with insights into future trends and strategic objectives. From the emergence of agentic AI and distributed systems to the cross-cultural

DOI: 10.1201/9781003674887-8

applicability of HR technologies, the argument was made that the future state of HR will depend largely on how organizations choose to act responsibly and inclusively with the adoption of new tools. The chapter emphasized maintaining a global and ethical perspective to maximize the benefits of AI-enabled HR innovations for diverse workforces across the world.

All the chapters, taken together, offer a detailed perspective on how generative AI can be applied to reinvent HR management. There are numerous opportunities—to support productivity, personalization, and innovation—but success will depend on integrating responsibility with efficiency. Ethical considerations, transparent decision-making, and global applicability should always be considered in any actionable AI strategy in HR. This book offers a pragmatic playbook and critical lens for the opportunities and challenges ahead. As HR professionals, leaders, and organizations embark on this journey, one guiding principle must be clear: generative AI is not simply about replacing human tasks—it is about amplifying human capacity, generating equity, and preparing workplaces for the future.

Table 8.1 provides a concise overview of how every chapter reflects on the role played by generative AI in contemporary HR management. Chapter 1 presents the background of generative AI, describing its development, advantages, and potential to improve productivity in HR systems. Chapter 2 addresses recruitment, detailing how AI solutions minimize job postings, automate resume screening, and customize candidate engagement, ultimately enhancing efficiency and fairness. Chapter 3 continues this evolution to onboarding and training, illustrating how AI-based learning platforms ensure customized development and ongoing skill advancement.

TABLE 8.1
Summary of Key Insights

Chapter	Core Focus	Key Takeaways
Role of generative AI in HR	Foundations of AI in HR	Defined GenAI, compared to traditional AI, highlighted productivity gains, financial implications for SMEs.
GenAI transforming HR	Recruitment and candidate experience	AI for job postings, resume screening, bias reduction, and personalized candidate journeys.
Onboarding and training	Employee success	AI-driven onboarding, adaptive learning, predictive analytics for skills.
Engagement and retention	Employee growth	Personalized engagement, career mapping, succession planning.
Implementing AI in HR	Strategy and operations	Steps to prepare, integrate, and manage AI adoption; importance of team readiness.
Ethical and legal frontiers	Responsible AI	Bias, privacy, compliance issues; best practices for ethical, transparent AI.
Future trends and insights	Strategic foresight	Agentic and distributed AI, cross-cultural adoption, global perspectives on HR AI.

Chapter 4 focuses on employee engagement and retention, with an emphasis on the ability of AI to personalize communication, recognition, and career development approaches. Chapter 5 offers an actionable implementation roadmap—readiness assessment, tool integration, and change management—while highlighting the need for cultural flexibility and team training. Chapter 6 looks to ethics and legality, addressing bias, privacy, and regulatory compliance while promoting open and ethical AI systems. Finally, Chapter 7 delves into upcoming trends such as agentic and distributed AI and cross-cultural adoption to visualize a globally inclusive future of AI in HR.

Overall, the table encapsulates the book's central message: generative AI is revolutionizing HR as a data-driven, ethical, and human-focused field—augmenting productivity and innovation while maintaining fairness, trust, and inclusivity.

8.1 VISUALIZING THE HR LIFECYCLE WITH GENERATIVE AI

The conceptual map shown in Figure 8.1 outlines the overall integration of generative AI into the HR lifecycle. It begins at the recruitment stage, where AI helps optimize job postings and automates the screening process of resumes to increase efficiency and promote fairness. Onboarding follows, with AI systems enhancing processes and personalizing the orientation of employees. Engagement becomes the focus as employees acclimate to their roles, and AI helps design personalized strategies for communication, recognition, and professional development, which improves satisfaction and retention.

At the organizational level, considerations of ethics must also be addressed—bias mitigation, privacy protection, compliance with regulations—and these are all encompassed in the notion of trust and transparency in AI-led organizational HR decision-making. Finally, the lifecycle looks toward the future, both in terms of upcoming

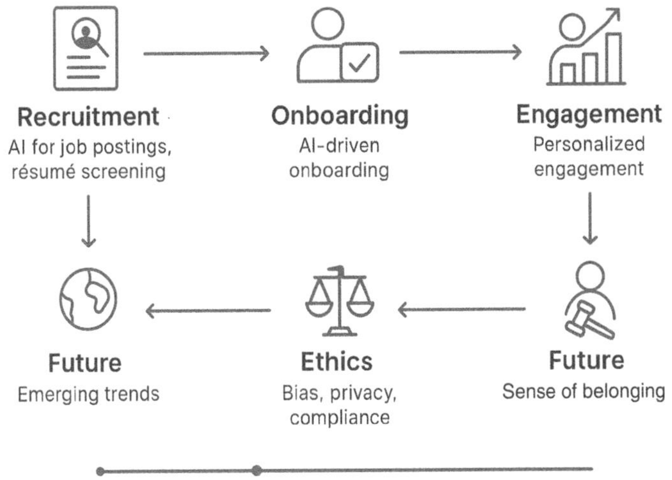

FIGURE 8.1 Generative AI for HR management.

trends such as agentic AI, distributed intelligence, and global adaptations as they emerge to define the next evolution of human resource management (HRM).

In total, the flow implies that generative AI in HR is not a set of tools; rather, it represents a continuous process that is interlinked and provides increased efficiency while maintaining ethical and human-centered values.

Index

Pages in *italics* refer to figures and pages in **bold** refer to tables.

I

J

K

L

M

N

O

P

U

V

W

X